PENGUIN BOOKS

My Time

My Time

How to make the rest of life the **best of life**

JOAN BAKER & MANDY FEALY

PENGUIN BOOKS

PENGUIN BOOKS
Published by the Penguin Group
Penguin Group (NZ), 67 Apollo Drive, Rosedale,
North Shore 0632, New Zealand (a division of Pearson New Zealand Ltd)
Penguin Group (USA) Inc., 375 Hudson Street,
New York, New York 10014, USA
Penguin Group (Canada), 90 Eglinton Avenue East, Suite 700, Toronto,
Ontario, M4P 2Y3, Canada (a division of Pearson Penguin Canada Inc.)
Penguin Books Ltd, 80 Strand, London, WC2R 0RL, England
Penguin Ireland, 25 St Stephen's Green,
Dublin 2, Ireland (a division of Penguin Books Ltd)
Penguin Group (Australia), 250 Camberwell Road, Camberwell,
Victoria 3124, Australia (a division of Pearson Australia Group Pty Ltd)
Penguin Books India Pvt Ltd, 11, Community Centre,
Panchsheel Park, New Delhi – 110 017, India
Penguin Books (South Africa) (Pty) Ltd, 24 Sturdee Avenue,
Rosebank, Johannesburg 2196, South Africa

Penguin Books Ltd, Registered Offices: 80 Strand, London, WC2R 0RL, England

First published by Penguin Group (NZ), 2011
1 3 5 7 9 10 8 6 4 2

Copyright © Joan Baker and Mandy Fealy, 2011

The right of Joan Baker and Mandy Fealy to be identified as the authors of this
work in terms of section 96 of the Copyright Act
1994 is hereby asserted.

Designed and typeset by Pindar, NZ
Printed in Australia by McPherson's Printing Group

ISBN 9780143565734

A catalogue record for this book is available
from the National Library of New Zealand.

www.penguin.co.nz

Contents

Introduction

_____

'This time, like all times, is a very good one,
if we but know what to do with it.'
Ralph Waldo Emerson

Are you yearning for more time for you? Time for you to do what you want, when you want, and with the people you care about? That's My Time. Most of us are really ready to live our lives to the full. We want to play and work and be healthy and be challenged. It's time for My Time.

We have been talking to lots of babyboomers about life after work. That's life beyond the fulltime work that most of us have to do for thirty or forty years. Most of our interviewees are approaching the end of this work period; others are beyond that point. We wanted to find out how people are thinking and feeling about getting near the end of fulltime work. We also wanted to know what those who had already passed the official retirement point thought: what was life like for them, what did they wish they had done differently, what advice would they pass on to others? We were looking for sage advice and some common sense, some practical ways to enhance your My Time – because that's what it is: time for you. The one thing that almost all interviewees agreed on is that they wanted their lives to be wonderful. How they defined wonderful varied enormously. This book is about making sure that you know how to create your own customised version of My Time.

According to our interviewees, we babyboomers want to do what we want to do and when we want to do it. The list may be long and varied; it's certainly different from previous generations. If the idea of 'me' and 'My Time' strikes you as selfish or self-indulgent, think again. The people we interviewed all spoke of spending more time with family, helping others, giving back to society or making a contribution in some way.

> According to our interviewees, we babyboomers want to do what we want to do and when we want to do it.

Allowing for all of the wonder of individual differences, we babyboomers approaching retirement or already retired from fulltime work share many characteristics. Most of us are acutely conscious that it's time to 'stop getting ready to get ready', as one interviewee put it, and get on with living our lives to the full. That's because we have a new sense of passing time. Already we know people in our age group who have had their lives upended by serious health problems and other calamities. We no longer feel the immunities of youth – we know we're mortal and we'd better get on with things. We start to 'get real' about many aspects of life. Some of the facades start to erode – there is less need to pursue ambition, to accumulate material proof of wealth, and we become more truthful with ourselves and each other.

We meet many individuals in our work who are contemplating a big change or longing for a different life. But many struggle with working out how to make the good life happen – whether it's a major career shift, stepping off the corporate ladder entirely or creating a whole new portfolio of work and lifestyle options. Most of us seem wired up to spend much more time yearning than preparing, but our observation is that you need to attend to some key things if you are to get the change you want – and on terms you will like. Many struggle with working out just how to make the different way of life they yearn for happen. It's not enough to keep your head down, your bottom up, work your heart out and hope it will all come right. Yeah, right!

Is this book for you? Well, if you're happy with what you are doing and how you are living your life we are delighted for you and possibly have little extra to offer. However, if you have a sneaking suspicion that there could be more, that this life you are leading cannot be 'it', or if you want to make sure the rest of your life is lived more on your terms and that you get some good My Time, then this is definitely the book for you. You may be relatively young but seeking to make a big change – become self-employed, perhaps – or older and seeking a complete lifestyle with elements of work for pure satisfaction or just to supplement income. Wherever you are at, according to our interviewees, there are many things to consider and work through.

If you choose to do nothing, little may change except that you will get older and lose more of your options as time passes. You may also leave yourself at the mercy of the winds of change – outdated skills, unaccommodating employers, outmoded thinking, unhealthy practices. Is the life you are leading worth the price you are paying – or will pay – to lead it? Many of life's greatest tragedies occur when we give up what we want most for what we are willing to settle for now.

Making change is exciting for some of us; a little scary for the rest of us. But no matter how many more decades you expect to have, you owe it to yourself and those you love to have the rest of life as the best of life – and now. It's never too early to get My Time. It's almost never too late.

We hope as you read on that you will quickly run out of excuses for why you are not living the

> We hope as you read on that you will quickly run out of excuses for why you are not living the life you want.

life you want. There's no need to wait for an official 'retirement' age – you can change whenever you decide. You have earned the right to be who you are, to have at least some of what you want and to spend your time doing meaningful things. This immediately raises questions about who you might be, what is it that you want and how you could live in a way that is more meaningful for you – and, of course, how to make that happen.

Now.

Joan Baker
Mandy Fealy

www.mytime.co.nz
contact@my-time.co.nz

My Time
In Today's
World

'Design your life. Then live it.'
Elizabeth Schneider

Quiz: Do you need more My Time?

How many of these questions can you answer 'yes' to?

1　Are you working at stuff you have to do rather than what you want to do?

2　Do you struggle to spend as much time with loved ones as you'd like?

3　Are you bored, underchallenged or understimulated?

4　Are you overweight because you have poor eating habits?

5　Are you unfit because you have poor exercise habits?

6　Is your sleep poor because you are stressed or unhealthy?

7　Are you going through life rather than getting the life you want?

8　Are you more stressed than is comfortable for you?

9　Does your family have difficulty accepting or living within a budget?

10　Are you still carrying debt (mortgage, loans, credit card)?

11　Are you worried about your financial future?

12　Do you feel that you'll never be able to give up working a great deal?

13　Are you worried about the future in general?

14 Are you afraid that you'll die with your song unsung?

15 Do you feel unfulfilled?

16 Have you very little time to pursue things you are interested in?

17 Do you find it difficult to do any voluntary work?

18 Have you set aside the dreams of your youth?

19 Do you lack a great network of friends and acquaintances outside of work?

20 Are you without an exciting dream and plan for your future?

The more of these you say yes to, the more you need some My Time!

1–5 Just need a tune up. Congratulations! You sound like you are well on the way to getting lots of My Time. Review the areas where you still need to make changes and read on to find some ideas about making your life even better.

6–10 Need a little work. You have obviously started on the journey to getting at least some of what really matters to you. However, there are still lots of areas where you do not have a good balance. Check to see if there is a cluster of problems, eg, self-care such as exercise, sleep and nutrition. Identify what's not working for you and look at the chapters that can help.

11–15 High time for My Time. You sound like you are not enjoying much of what life could offer. It's likely that you are dissatisfied with your work, having very little fun outside of work and are taking little care of yourself. We have lots of ideas to help you put this right and put the zest back into your life. Read on.

16–20 Urgent! We are worried about you! You seem to have a miserable mix – little choice or stimulation at work, poor habits for looking after yourself, little or no fun and low expectations for the future. We're here to help. Drop everything else and read on – you really need to get some My Time and fast!

Debunking myths

Many myths abound concerning life after work. Nearly all of them are negative. Nearly all of them are wrong. The way we think about things has a profound effect on the way we feel. In some cases our thoughts are paralysing. This is all the more troublesome when there is no real basis for our beliefs but they are driving our behaviour anyway.

> **Many myths abound concerning life after work. Nearly all of them are negative.**

If any of these myths we're about to look at are worrying you or holding you back from getting the life you want, it's time to ditch them. Replace them with some facts that actually support you in leading the kind of lifestyle you want. Our myths are very powerful inhibitors – what we tell ourselves becomes the truth. So, watch your self-talk and think again! Challenge those negative habits of your mind.

Which myths do you subscribe to?

Myth. You are on the scrapheap.

Only if you agree. There have never been so many options for those who have finished fulltime work. You can continue to work for as long as you wish to in a number of different ways.

> **Angus**, in his seventies, now chairs the board of the business he left as chief executive. He's a director on several other boards and trusts as well. He mentors people he considers high potential and is generous with his time and energy to numerous causes and individuals. He barely has time to fit in his winter sports and frequent trips overseas to 'keep up' with both business associates and scattered family members. Oh, and the grandchildren!

Myth. You are too old.

No you are not. Given today's life expectancies you are probably only about two thirds of the way through life. And there is some real truth to fifty being the new forty and sixty being the new fifty and so on – our better health and vigour means that many retirees are in great shape and certainly not old.

> There is some real truth to fifty being the new forty and sixty being the new fifty.

> **Paula**, in her eighties, has just returned from Turkey. She had lived in that part of the world earlier and, as you do, had taught herself the language. Indomitable in spirit and attitude, she intends to continue to travel the world as long as she can. She's slim, fit, lively and attractive – and well informed about the world. Companions, keep up, please!

Myth. Retirees don't work.

Actually more and more of them do, and through choice. Retirement used to mean no longer at work – that was almost the definition of retirement. Nowadays, however, as we are healthier and fitter when we finish fulltime work and as we expect to live for a few decades rather than a few years, more and more people work. Some feel they must if they want to retain their standard of living; others do so because they want all the other benefits of work.

> **Janet** held many senior executive roles before she'd had enough and opted for My Time. As regional president for a major service organisation she now works as long and hard as ever but with renewed zest. Her not-for-profit (NFP) work takes her around the country and representing NZ overseas. She's working very hard to modernise the organisation and give it new relevance for the twenty-first century.

Myth. You lack up-to-date skills.

Well, if it's true for you, it shouldn't be! And it's nothing to do with retiring. In fact, it simply begs the question of what you are going to do about your skill levels.

> **Ray** is a 'retired' farmer. He'd had enough of being tied to the place 24/7, finding it very hard to even get a family holiday each year. Much as he wanted his My Time, he was in no way ready to stand by and watch agriculture leave him behind. With the skills he acquired over several decades he has organised syndicates to buy several farms and he chairs the board that oversees them.

Gumboots are just for farm visits now! Oh, and did we mention that he has used these farming skills to invest in high tech agri-business and open corporate doors for sales?

Myth. You can't learn new things.

The brain is plastic. You can teach the old dog new tricks.

> **Nancy** worked all of her life in the 'sensible and safe' profession of teaching, having set aside her first love, which was art. My Time for her was spent learning Chinese and resuming her painting . . . just because she could. She has learned enough Chinese to communicate easily on her travels to China and is supplementing her pension with income generated from the sale of her artwork.

Myth. Aging means decline.

Research shows that this assumption is self-fulfilling. But adequate exercise, mental challenge and ongoing participation in the world keep decline at bay.

> **Jim** is well into his sixties but still alpine climbing up things the rest of us only see from aeroplanes! Not only is he spectacularly fit (there's a reason most climbers are in their twenties and thirties), he also has the resilience (mental and emotional) that it takes to tackle the world's highest peaks.

Myth. You are unproductive.

There's no evidence at all that older people are unproductive. Quite the contrary. Older people often have additional skills and experience that make them more productive – they may have developed better people skills, they have more experience to use in anticipating problems and they often have better networks to assist in getting things done. Unless your job is highly physical – and few are today – age is unlikely to be a factor in your productivity.

> Older people often have additional skills and experience that make them more productive.

Dave retired from his chief executive role well over a decade ago. Since then he has done several terms as a city councillor and run an extensive property portfolio. He also manages to consult to businesses and is valued for his ability to get to the heart of the matter in double quick time. His extensive experience gives him perspective and good judgement. His valuable network means he can get complicated issues resolved – fast!

Myth. Your brain doesn't work well.

Again, the evidence is against the myth. We know the brain continues to work well as long as it is used.

Terence was a well known hospital specialist in his day. Two decades after his official retirement he was still poring through every new copy of the *Lancet* as soon as it arrived. It didn't pay to argue with him – on any subject! His formidable intellect, fed on a steady diet of up-to-date information, meant that he held most of the cards in any debate!

Myth. Creative people are special and are born creative.

Creative people are made, not born. You can unleash your creativity at any stage of life.

> **Gayle** has always liked music. However, in addition to playing very well she has recently turned her hand to composing scores for film. Not content with this display of 'generativity' she has also decided to write a local history – because the existing ones are neither comprehensive nor engaging enough!

Myth. We only grieve over death.

We grieve over many things in life, for example, leaving school and childhood, even though we may be excited about the next stage. Transitions usually bring losses as well as gains: we might grieve about leaving home, or even about getting married and so losing some of our independence. Roads not taken, failures, opportunities missed, may all be grieved over.

> Roads not taken, failures, opportunities missed, may all be grieved over.

> **Annette** comes from a boisterous family of seven. It might have been fun for the kids growing up together but, as the oldest, Annette was mindful of what life was like for her mother. An excellent student, she resolved early on to focus on

her medical career and remain childfree. In her early fifties now, though she is successful professionally and happily partnered, she is tearful. And yet she would make the same choice again. Such is grief.

Myth. Life after work will be great.

My Time can be all about doing what you want when you want and with the people you wish – but that's much more likely if you prepare your mind, body, wallet and soul for it. We're seeing people who make the preparation to get My Time on their terms but also some who think it will all just happen. We don't.

That's what this book is about – not only changing the 'what' in your life but also how to make it happen now.

Retirement then and now

What led us to write a book about My Time? We're babyboomers too. Over recent years many of our clients have been asking for advice on retirement or claiming that retirement is not for them. As they look forward all are asking 'What next?' Our parents' concept of retirement doesn't work for most babyboomers. Why not? Well, retirement is a relatively new idea. Take a look at history. It's not so long ago that few of us lived long enough for retirement to be a consideration – people worked hard, wore out, sickened perhaps and died, and all of that in fairly short order. For most people life was nasty, brutal and short. Even a century ago, you were doing well to live much beyond sixty. Those who did survive for longer had roles looking after grandchildren, preparing food and minding the fire while the stronger ones worked. Older people were dependent on their families once they could no longer work.

Until quite recently work was likely to be physically demanding and often unhealthy – heavy, cold, wet and dirty. Much of it was done outdoors or in appalling factories. The typical retiree had worked fulltime for the same employer for thirty to forty years. He (and it was usually a he) retired with a gold watch (if he was lucky) and spent his remaining years gardening, reading the paper, golfing and indulging grandchildren. Nobody seemed much concerned with what he (or she!) thought of this arrangement; if we thought of it at all, we concluded that they were having a well-earned rest. Retirement was often synonymous with leisure (and we were often very tired or worn out and needed the rest).

Retirement originated as a way of creating positions for younger workers. The pension was introduced in the mid twentieth century but did not make much of a demand on the state coffers, as few lived long enough to enjoy it. The drive to introduce welfare states after the Depression and two world wars changed the retirement landscape. Ironically, we are now retiring healthy, vigorous people, when we are short of workers in many areas. Countries have huge pension liabilities as retired workers can be expected to live for decades. As we are seeing at the moment, many countries around the world are debating raising their official retirement age as smaller cohorts of younger workers struggle to fund the huge numbers of babyboomer retirees.

The old idea of retirement at sixty-five is now a very different retirement, because generally people are healthier when they enter their fifties and sixties and have access to better care as they age. Many of us will have almost as many years after fulltime work as we spent in a fulltime job. Work today is much more likely to centre on information than physical strength. Health and safety in the workplace is a dominant concern, and we are likely to have fewer injuries and work-related diseases; and while our work may be emotionally demanding or even stressful, it is rarely physically debilitating.

> **Many of us will have almost as many years after fulltime work as we spent in a fulltime job.**

Retirement for many now simply means a change of employer or employment. Many who are compulsorily retired from one role simply find another in a similar – or altogether different – field. They may well choose to do different work or to work differently – on contract, part time, seasonally or in a voluntary capacity. Few stop entirely and retire to the La-Z-Boy recliner. Even if they are financially comfortable, many don't want a life of just leisure. Others find that they cannot have the lifestyle they want without doing some paid work.

Nowadays, women's life expectancy is in the mid eighties (in fact 2010 research is predicting 50 per cent of women in America will live to 100), and men's is just below this. With healthcare improving all the time, predictions are for these figures to rise over the next few decades. We now expect the state to assist with a basic retirement income and for the individual to provide the rest through lifetime savings. It's unusual in our society for the retired to live with or be dependent on their families for shelter and food.

We think it's very interesting that those who can afford to retire (as in, do no work at all) are the least likely to. The successful, the educated and the well off seem more and more determined to fill these years with interesting and meaningful work – chairing boards, acting as directors for business and nonprofit organisations, consulting, coaching, volunteering – what they call giving back. The reason is simple: these people love what they do and they still have the energy and the will to do it. They simply adapt their drive and skills and continue to contribute. Sure, they may take more trips and enjoy a bit more leisure and flexibility than they had in their former roles but their lives are still demanding and full. They drive the agenda and the timetable. They have the choice to do what they want to do, when they want to do it. My Time.

> We think it's very interesting that those who can afford to retire are the least likely to.

What's wrong
with retirement?

To retire means to withdraw. That might have made sense when your life expectancy was only a few years more than the normal age for retirement, or if you were worn out from the rigours of physical or back-breaking work. Retirement usually means that we have given up our fulltime occupation, ie, work. This makes work the central issue. The implication is that people do not wish to work, or that the workplace no longer welcomes them. Both notions are often far from the truth. Most of the people we have interviewed who are retired continue to work hard – at a variety of things. Some are working fulltime, others part time, in paid work. Most of the others are working very hard at something – not-for-profit work, projects of their own, sporting activities, learning pursuits or greater involvement with family. There is no suggestion at all that they wish to avoid work; quite the contrary.

Retirement used to imply fulltime leisure – usually spent in fairly gentle pursuits like gardening, bowls and pottering in the shed. Leisure is still very important to babyboomers – in fact they seek more of it, while still working. However, few people that we talk to want a life of nothing but leisure. Rather, most are seeking to continue to make a contribution and live a life filled with purposeful activity. Yes, My Time is really important. It's not selfish, as it means active engagement with a wide range of age groups, working, giving back and filling useful roles, paid and unpaid. Retirement now seems to mean getting much more My Time, rather than no longer working.

> **Many people are looking to make a major lifestyle change earlier.**

Many people are looking to make a major lifestyle change earlier – we see people in their thirties, forties and fifties who wish to live life differently. That can mean lots of things:

- change of career
- change of pace
- self-employment
- business ownership
- a switch to not-for-profit work
- a rural location
- a lifestyle choice for the whole family.

Not everybody wants to retire, but many yearn for more My Time, more freedom to do their own thing. And some form of work is likely to be a component of that.

Our findings show that people who are contemplating some form of 'retirement' are very busy researching and preparing for it.

Our changing world

It's easy to get trapped in static thinking. When we look back we have no difficulty seeing the trends and major changes in our lifetime, as hindsight is a wonderful thing. We see, for example, more women entering the workforce, rising prosperity for the educated, more knowledge work, the availability and affordability of conveniences such as microwaves and dishwashers, cellphones and the internet. However, we find it much more difficult – and often we are more reluctant – to look forward and see the signs of changes that will have an effect in the decades to come. It seems easier to accommodate the changes around us than to anticipate what might be coming over the hill and having an impact on our lives. How many of us are refusing to accept social networking sites such as Facebook? Are we right – hoping, perhaps, that it will disappear?! Or will we be left out, left behind?

Why does this matter? Well, we will probably still be alive for decades. Our world is unlikely to remain as is; in fact most pundits agree that the rate of change itself is accelerating. It's therefore really important to keep an eye on the futures that are unfolding, as we are going to inhabit that world and need to prepare for it. In retrospect, it was obvious by the beginning of the 1990s that technology was changing our world. The very young readily embraced it if they could afford to (remember how much those early mobiles and PCs cost!), while many of us who were already well into our thirties were more resistant. After all, using a computer required you to learn DOS! It wasn't easy – and maybe it would go away. Looking back now, we may wish we had embraced new ways of doing things faster. Think of what is happening today: you probably use text messages and email. However, it is less likely you are a big blogger or tweeter, and Facebook may be something you are only just warming to – and only because it means you can communicate with your children.

> But it's also critical that we maintain a flexible outlook, given that we are likely to be around for a lot of the future.

The future is unknowable, by definition. That can lead to a belief that there's no point in preparing for it at all. We beg to differ. Yes, it's important to live in the now, and to look after yourself well. But it's also critical that we maintain a flexible outlook, given that we are likely to be around for a lot of the future. One of the best ways to remain flexible in mind and attitude is to continue to scan the future for signs of what's to come. Embrace the new ideas.

We are already in the second decade of the twenty-first century. The signs of what's to come are already lining up on the horizon. What does it look like, and what are the implications for the next few decades?

Political/legal implication. Governments all over the Western world are struggling to meet pension commitments. There are attempts everywhere to raise the official retirement age. Mandatory retirement from work is increasingly being legislated against. And 'ageism' is raising its head as the newest -ism. The landscape is changing. Populations are aging – there will be proportionally more older people in most Western countries than ever before in the next few decades. This is likely to lead to many changes as these people will have significant voting power, and, what's more, they actually vote.

Economic implication. There will be fewer and fewer younger people paying taxes to help pay for the aging babyboomers – perhaps leading to intergenerational conflict. It may also revive the argument for capital gains tax as it may otherwise be very difficult to get sufficient contribution from those no longer working fulltime. Much of the wealth will be concentrated in the hands of babyboomers, leading to changes in spending patterns and demand for different goods and services. Many Western economies may struggle to find enough skilled workers to replace the big babyboomer cohort as they cease fulltime work – this may inflate wages and salaries, or lead to calls for greater immigration quotas, or it may push much work offshore to lower-cost countries.

Environmental implication. We are already acutely conscious of environmental issues facing our planet. It's likely that we will see both legislative changes and increasing social pressure in this area in coming years. Many people who are contemplating more leisure time plan to travel. What if international travel is priced very high because of carbon consumption or we are allocated a personal allowance? The real cost of some of our behaviour – our obsession with personal vehicles, big houses, our profligate use of power – may well be brought home to us at a personal level sooner rather than later. Recent natural disasters have also highlighted how our expectations can change in a heartbeat.

Social implication. It is already clear that our society is changing a great deal. There will be more older people and fewer younger ones. There is more and more demand for dwellings for singles and older couples; and at the other extreme, there is a need for housing to accommodate blended and extended families.

Technology implication. While it is tempting to dismiss much of what we hear as sci-fi, there are huge technological changes imminent. There are spectacular breakthroughs in medicine, for example in stem cell research. Communications technology – which has in large part redefined how we live over the last twenty years – has further to go, with handheld devices allowing us to do just about anything we wish from our chairs, anywhere in the world. The tyrannies of time and distance are being lifted. Almost all of these changes are particularly advantageous for older people as they optimise our wisdom and wealth and minimise the need for physical energy or even our physical presence.

> All of these changes are particularly advantageous for older people as they optimise our wisdom and wealth.

My Time Dreaming

'The future belongs to those who believe
in the beauty of their dreams.'

Eleanor Roosevelt

What do you want?

It's deceptively easy to ask that question, but often hard to answer it. Easy for the small stuff: What do you want for breakfast? What would you like to do this evening? Where do you want to go for the weekend break? You might dither, even debate, but they are relatively simple choices. However, what do you really want in your life, for your life, for yourself, for your loved ones, for the rest of your life? These are big questions, and they are often avoided. People find these questions too big, too confronting, too overwhelming, and it's easier to put them in the too hard basket. Not surprising really, as we have very little practice at answering such questions. Apart from a few very wealthy individuals, most human beings over the course of history have been focused on mere survival – the question of what you might like or want was irrelevant. We babyboomers are a very privileged generation, but we don't have many role models for scoping out an ideal life for ourselves. Yes, we're aching for more My Time – but how to decide what to do with it?

We all daydream and fantasise, but that's easy and rarely confronts us with any of the hard choices. You might say you'd like to give up your job. But do you really want to give up all work, forever? You might say you'd like to live somewhere else – better weather, less traffic, more lifestyle. But do you want to sell your home, move away from family and friends, develop new colleagues, relationships and associations?

If you are dissatisfied with your current life or you are facing a major forced transition such as redundancy or compulsory retirement, then it's really important to spend plenty of time considering what you really really want. You only have to get a very few things right in your life – and among those is figuring out what is important for you. Otherwise you risk applying all of your life's efforts to chasing the wrong goals. What a waste!

Of course, what's really hard about all this, once you take it seriously, is that you have to consider what you will be giving up. All change is about moving from one state or situation to another. To make a fundamental change in your life you have to be prepared to give up some of who and what you are, in order to become more of who you could be and get what you really want.

> **Rich and Kate** had lived overseas for decades. They went where the jobs took them and both of them were in demand in senior management roles – Richard in telecommunications and Kate in finance. At one level they were 'living the dream' – big salaries, wonderful living conditions (albeit in an apartment in Asia), fabulous holidays . . . when they could get any time off. All the rewards that they had worked so hard to get began to pall – they were exhausted, the travel was incessant, there was no time for anything but work. They decided to 'ease back'. Neither wanted to give up work forever – they were far too vigorous for that. They decided to go 'cold turkey' and return to New Zealand. There was no prospect of doing what they normally worked at, as they decided to live in a beautiful but relatively small coastal centre. The big incomes had to go, new challenges had to be found, and

life had to be rebuilt in a completely new location. Five years down the track all is going well – they are back to manageable but busy lives, and are healthier and happier. My Time achieved.

What you're over and do not want!

It might seem perverse to ask what you don't want when you are trying to figure out what you really do want. However, one of the lessons you learn as life goes on is finding out what you don't like, what doesn't work for you and what you never ever want in your life again! Does that ring any bells for you? With over 100 years of experience between the two of us we have learned the hard way about lots of things we don't want in our lives – certain kinds of work, particular sorts of people, situations or life circumstances that we are determined never to experience again.

Because we all bring lots of life experience to this task it's often much easier to work out what you don't want, which then points you in the direction of the things you feel you must have in order to be happy. As you identify what you wish to avoid you become much clearer about what you have to bring into being in order to have more pleasure, happiness and meaning.

Let's talk about relationships. Both of us have had the unhappy experiences of separation and divorce. We have learned a great deal about how important it is to have supportive and enriching partners in our lives. Needless to say, we have also learned a great deal about what it takes for good relationships to endure – but more about that later. We would both say that we definitely do not want poor close relationships and, by extension, we really do want caring, mature, responsible people in our lives. So for example you might say, based on your own experiences, you don't want a partner who is:

- negative
- selfish
- uncaring about others in general
- disrespectful of you
- dishonest

And extrapolating from that, you are seeking to have someone in your life who is:

- positive and enthusiastic
- kind and generous
- caring and helpful
- respectful of others
- full of integrity
- fun.

Fun is a biggie! Make sure you clarify what counts for you.

Our research has made it very clear to us that your health is key to the quality of your life whatever age you are. For most of our lives, each of us has been almost inexhaustible. We had endless energy and used it to the full. Having experienced poor health at times, we have no difficulty deciding that being optimally healthy – physically, mentally and emotionally – is high up on the list of 'must haves'. Just think how, with a stomach bug or a bout of flu, we can lose the energy to get up and go. Being unwell steals from us any desire we have for other parts of our lives. So if you are very clear that you do not want to be emotionally burned out, mentally exhausted and physically unfit, then you may find it much easier to specify that your dream life would allow you to be:

- physically exercised
- eating healthily
- sleeping well
- mentally calm but stimulated
- emotionally secure and content.

Ditto with work. We can understand that some people might wish never to do any work again. There are certainly kinds of work (and managers! and colleagues!) we would make sure we avoid. Having said that, we know that we both want some challenging work and projects (paid or unpaid) for the rest of our days. You might well clarify that you do not wish to:

- work weekends
- travel a lot for work
- be at the whim of an unappreciative boss
- be micromanaged
- do overly routine work
- be told what to do and when to do it
- take on so much that you have no My Time

. . . and so become clearer that you do want:

- some autonomy and self-direction
- flexible work hours

- the ability to work from home some of the time
- stimulating, challenging work.

It is easier to avoid what you don't want if you are clear about what's on the list. This works for every important aspect of life. Knowing what you wish to avoid makes it simpler to decide what you certainly want. The clearer you are, the easier it is to bring that into being. We make little choices all the time, and if you know what you want you will find it much easier to flow in that direction.

Why should you change anything? There's no point in making a change unless it's for the better. What would be better for you if you were leading a different kind of life, a life that gave you more My Time?

Among the things that drive us to make changes are:

- being able to spend more time with family who live overseas
- getting more control over our annual, and daily, timetables
- having more choice over the work we do
- having more time to read and learn
- being able to better manage our health
- having time to do our own thing
- looking after close family
- spending more time outdoors
- skiing when the conditions are ideal
- giving children more attention
- doing not-for-profit work
- exploring new interests
- travelling more
- doing more challenging work
- enjoying more variety
- having opportunities to grow and learn
- having the freedom to do several things at once.

So what's stopping you?

Why don't you just do what you want?
Why don't you have life on your terms?
What's stopping you?
What are the hurdles you need to overcome?

Talking to our interviewees, we have found that many of them feel 'blocked' by one or more of the following fears:

Money.

Concerns about money – or rather not having enough of it – dominate. Even many who have accumulated quite a lot of wealth in the form of property and superannuation are worried that they won't have enough to 'see them through'. For some people, of course, because of their personalities, there is no 'enough'. It's not that they have a figure that they can't meet – some won't even set a figure – but they are convinced they won't have enough to be secure. The irony is that, depending on how you wish to live after fulltime work, it may not cost as much as you think, and you may already have more than you need. Remember that there is an entire industry out there trying to convince you that you need more – and that they are the answer to your problem!

Being sidelined.

Fears about being old, unwanted, redundant and useless stop many people from considering the end of their fulltime work and planning for the next phase. Not working does not make you old. Many so-called retirees still work, for money or unpaid. Many are still in great demand professionally. Fears of being sidelined tend to come from the mental pictures we have of our parents' generation – so it pays to remind yourself that this is not your parents' retirement.

> Not working does not make you old. Many so-called retirees still work, for money or unpaid.

Others' opinion.

We spend a huge amount of our lives being asked who we are and what we do. Some people worry about what they will say when they've finished fulltime work. We find more and more people are happy to call themselves retired (the younger the better) and wear it as a badge of honour, even with smugness. Of course they are mostly the ones who are still engaged fully with life and have plenty of interesting tales to tell. You may not care what others think; but if you do, it's worth coming up with a good story to tell people. We all have many identities, and are so much more than our job title.

Self-esteem.

For many of us, our sense of self-worth is tied up in what we do. This may well be more true of men than women – as yet it is rare for women to have worked fulltime all of their lives and to identify with their careers as much as many men appear to do, though that's changing rapidly. However, if you have always seen yourself as a farmer, a doctor, a marketer, a journalist, a manager or an engineer, then it can be very challenging to think about who you will be when you stop doing whatever it is you do.

The unknown.

It's often said that it's much harder to move away from something than to move towards something else. The new life may well be much better than the earlier one, but people are (and rightly so) quite cautious about change and too many unknowns. The clearer a picture you can get of what you are changing to, the less you'll fear change. It pays to reduce the number of unknowns.

Loneliness.

When most of your life has been built around your job and that's where you have spent most of your waking hours, it's natural to wonder if you will be bereft if you leave. After all, many of your friends may be work-based. You may fear that most of these people will have little time or interest in you once you leave.

Relationships.

Many people wonder what will happen to their closest relationships if they leave fulltime work. Over the years we all settle into our patterns and habits. He may be acutely aware that she has a busy life of her own. She has routines that do not include him. At a bigger level, people may fear that discussions about big changes may reveal very different desires for the future – he wants to spend large amounts of time fishing from a remote spot in the South Island and she wants to spend lots more time in Sydney with the grandchildren.

Our fears are many and varied, and often irrational. That does not make them less real. It's important to identify what exactly may be holding you back, because then you can get to work on dispelling the fear by taking action. You can do things to lower your risks (and hence your fear) about all of the above.

> Our fears are many and varied, and often irrational. That does not make them less real.

What do you dream of?

We hesitated to use the word 'vision' because so many of you may have had such a hollow and forgettable experience of creating corporate visions – many ending up on brass plaques in foyers, never to be enacted, and mostly referred to with cynicism by you and your colleagues. However, just because it's often badly done does not mean that it's not a good idea. We all daydream, and visions and dreams for the future – whether it's your own or an organisation's – are important because they create a compelling picture that you wish to achieve. It's not what the vision is that's important – it's what the vision does. When you have a clear vision about what you want to bring about, then it's much easier to get up and get going to make it happen. Clear visions and well articulated dreams are energising – they make us want to do whatever we need to make them a reality. When you know what you really want, it is easier to get out of bed, easier to tackle difficult situations and people, easier to stick to your plan. Time flies when you are filled with passion and excitement about whatever it is you wish to bring into your life. Capturing your dreams and realising them is what My Time is all about.

Your dream of My Time does not have to be grand: you do not

need to save the world, bring about global peace, or even end up filthy rich! You don't even have to be successful in the eyes of others – just in your own eyes. We don't think you can make your dream of the perfect life happen on demand, but we are convinced that if you spend time thinking, talking and reading you will become clearer about what really matters – what are the non-negotiables for you to have a great life. And remember that this does not all have to become clear at once. It's your dream and you can continue to shape it over time. What's important now is to begin to gather elements of the dream so that you can start to plan to make that dream come true. If you don't become clearer about what's on top you will risk blindly following someone else's plans for you – a better job, a further promotion, a bigger house, more lifestyle assets, more energy spent pursuing things that have little chance of making you happy, even though they might be right for someone else.

> If you don't become clearer about what's on top you will risk blindly following someone else's plans for you

You are unique. So don't borrow other people's dreams or plans (though by all means borrow their good ideas!). Start to think about what would make you feel like you had a great life. Consider aspects of life such as:

- relationships and family
- health and wellbeing
- work and income
- leisure and hobbies
- contribution and purpose
- learning and growth.

James was a professional golf coach working in Auckland. He liked his work and was good at his job. However, he felt that the pace of life demanded by the big city no longer suited him. He felt he spent far too much time in the car, and was under pressure at the golf club to do even more work as he was a favourite with members. James wanted to pull back into more My Time – to do less coaching, to have more time for the grandchildren. He also wanted to look after his own health better – while he looked trim and in great shape, he knew he was shortchanging his health by having too much stress and not enough variety in his life. He decided to move to a small South Island town and continue to coach golf but on a much reduced timetable. The long winters would ensure that there was time for other things – skiing, music, visiting family overseas and having the kids to stay.

No one else can tell you what's important to you; no one else can plan your life for you – though they may be able to help by talking through the issues and reminding you of when you are at your best and happiest. Unfortunately, none of us come with a manual! You are a 'sample of one' and you will have to make up your own manual, starting with the things you dream about.

Only you can say what would make for great My Time. It's not particularly realistic to expect your picture of a dream life to arrive fully formed. Rather, just as it is easier to specify aspects of life that you don't want, it's simpler to start compiling elements that you would like for the future.

Here are some that we hear about over and over. Use them to kick-start your thinking and begin your own list.

- a healthy level of physical fitness
- being near the sea
- a warm climate
- overseas travel

- 'enough' resources
- a new challenge
- being close to people you love
- having some purpose
- giving back to the community
- love
- simplicity
- making a difference.

Jenny was single and very happy and committed to her lifestyle. She ran an accounting and advisory business that filled her days, and delighted in her mortgage-free home. Her weekends were filled with walks, going to the beach, friends, and her interests of reading and films. She always bought season tickets to the ballet, opera and symphony orchestra. However, she worried constantly about her aging parents. They were doing okay and were still in their own home, but probably needed significantly more support than she could provide from afar. Jenny resolved the dilemma: she sold her home and her business. She moved to be near her parents. Their location was far from ideal for her skills, but she has managed to find a combination of contract work and the odd bit of consulting for small businesses. She's happy that this is perfect My Time for her – although to many outsiders she seems to have made big sacrifices for others. She's adamant that being true to her values – putting her family first – is what makes her happiest.

We have collected a veritable A to Z of the dozens of weird and wonderful things people are actually doing in their retirement – far too many to list here. They range from antiques and aeroclubs to zoology and everything in between, including boatbuilding, care for the terminally ill, crosswords, fencing, kiteboarding, knitting, nude limbo dancing . . . Get the picture? Those already in My Time are doing anything and everything from the mundane to the zany.

Discovering ideal My Time

How would your life look if you were living the life of your dreams? Where would you be? What would you be doing? Who would be with you? How would you spend your time? What would you be focusing on or engaged with?

We think it's helpful to ask yourself about your dreams from lots of different angles. Some questions resonate with one person, some with another. Dreaming is a serious business – after all, you are laying out a template for the rest of your life and will soon start to make concrete plans to achieve your vision. Who can support you in having these conversations with yourself? Some people may prefer to ponder all of this internally and only share with others when they are clear in their own mind. Others may find it helpful to discuss and debate the issues with friends and colleagues. Do whatever feels right for you, but make sure you commit plenty of time to the process. It does not matter to anyone else whether you put any of this in writing, but our experience is that it can help people to crystallise their thoughts.

> **We think it's helpful to ask yourself about your dreams from lots of different angles.**

Here are some techniques that you may find helpful.

Imagine that you are living the ideal life . . .

Where would you be? What would you be doing? Who would you be with? How would you spend your time? What would a typical day be like? Different people choose to write, draw, build a collage of images, compose a poem or whatever medium suits their style.

Assume you have won Lotto . . .

. . . and after you've spent a month on the beach in the Bahamas drinking cocktails with parasols, what would you do next, as money is not a problem?

Given only a year to live . . .

. . . how would you spend it?

10 Things I Want to Do Before I Die . . .

. . . what's on your 'bucket list'? Do you have a list of things you want to do?

Imagine you have twenty 'good' summers left . . .

. . . what will you do with them?

People spend far too little energy working out what really matters to them. Remember, you don't have to change the world. It's your My Time. You are in charge of determining what would be satisfying and fulfilling for you. Be wary of allowing others to set the agenda – your My Time dream does not have to be grand. Don't buy into what you feel you should want. It only has to be a good life for you. Good My Time is a highly customised design – remember that you are an experiment of one.

> You are in charge of determining what would be satisfying and fulfilling for you.

My Time Working

'The purpose of life is to discover your gift. The meaning of life is giving your gift away.'
David Viscott

The work question

Retirement used to mean the end of work, full stop. That made perfect sense when life expectancies were shorter, and when it was more usual for people to have retirement savings or superannuation that lasted for as long as they lived. This model no longer works for many reasons – some people need to supplement their savings, and many wish to continue working at least some of the time. Our interviewees had lots of reasons for seeking some further work. Which apply to you?

- I like to have some structure to my time
- I like the feeling of getting things done
- I enjoy socialising with work colleagues
- Work is a large part of who I am
- I like making a contribution
- I would miss the challenge
- Work forces me to learn and grow
- I feel part of the wider world when I'm at work

- I prefer work to leisure activities

- I look forward to tackling new problems

- The pros of work outweigh the cons

- Work keeps me feeling young and involved

- I don't want to lose touch with developments in my sector

- I don't want to lose touch with younger colleagues

- I'd rather be working than doing nothing

The more of these you agree with, the more it is likely that you would benefit from continuing to do some work. More My Time doesn't necessarily mean not working – it often just means putting work in its rightful place! And there's much more to work than the job you are leaving – it's perfectly possible to get many of the benefits of work without the downsides of a fulltime job. As indicated by the comments above, there are many psychological benefits from working. Whether or not you need or want the additional income, you may want to make sure that you replace some of these benefits in some way.

> **More My Time doesn't necessarily mean not working – it often just means putting work in its rightful place!**

Why work matters

Too many of us have been conditioned to see work as a negative: work is something unpleasant; something we are forced to do; the opposite of fun and play. And yet we have no difficulty talking of 'working' at our tennis game or golf swing or trying to grow perfect roses. Work at its most basic is simply effort. And effort is good for us.

Human beings don't seem to be programmed to do nothing; quite the contrary – we are constantly looking for meaningful achievement. We seem to respond well to having a purpose and goals. If we associate work only with the least attractive aspects of whatever we've been doing over the decades to earn a living, then we're missing the point. We've often wanted to spend less time at this 'work' and more time on our families, friends, hobbies and interests. The fact that we've had to work to feed our families and pay the mortgage makes it even less appealing – compulsion is never a good selling point.

> Work at its most basic is simply effort. And effort is good for us.

However, the alternative – which is doing nothing – is even less appealing. There is only so much leisure time a person can take – especially someone who is still vigorous in body and mind. Really, how much sport, shopping, gardening and unlimited SKY can you take?

Our experience is that meaningful activity is important to most people. Whether it is paid or not, you are likely to want – and even need – some form of work.

Work meets many of our most human needs:

It gives us something meaningful to do.

Only the most senseless of work is without purpose – choose something worthwhile.

It structures our efforts.

> After a lifetime of having too little time, it's a shame to replace it with having time to kill.

After a lifetime of having too little time, it's a shame to replace it with having time to kill. A measure of meaningful work gives us something to organise our other activities around and ensures we don't waste the rest of our days and weeks.

It keeps us connected.

We take for granted the people, skills and context of work while we are still there. Working at least a little keeps us aligned with the rest of the workforce and the real world.

It's challenging and stimulating.

Assuming that you choose something appropriate and interesting, you will be forced to keep apace and to continue to learn and grow.

> **You do not need to continue what you have been doing for the last twenty years.**

What needs does your work meet for you? Even if you have to take paid work because you need to supplement your income, it does not need to be a negative experience. You do not need to continue what you have been doing for the last twenty years. Most work is better than it ever was in the past, and you will have many advantages:

- There is a shortage of skilled and experienced people in many areas and industries.
- What you know and can do is much more important than your age and any physical requirements.
- Part-time and flexitime work is more readily available than in the past.
- It's easier to be a contractor or a worker from home than ever before.
- It is illegal for employers to discriminate based on age, gender or race.
- There is a greater range of work options than ever before.
- It's easier than ever to be self-employed.
- The internet and mobile technology enable many work options.

Will you work?

> It's often those who don't appreciate what work brings, other than dollars, who wish to be rid of work forever.

Increasingly, even those who are at formal retirement age are choosing to continue to do some work, paid or unpaid. Younger 'My Timers' almost all continue to work in some form. In fact, we find that the less people need to work, the more anxious they are to have all the advantages of work! It's often those who don't appreciate what work brings, other than dollars, who wish to be rid of work forever. Just another irony of life!

Most people who are seeking to leave the conventional fulltime job or business are seeking some kind of work. Which category fits you?

Self-employment: setting up a business, consulting, contracting, directing

Marcus fled Christchurch for Marlborough with his relatively young family several years ago. He's an experienced commercial lawyer but deliberately avoided a position with any of the law firms that were keen to snaffle him up. He practises alone, using a remote secretary. He is also director of a significant local business. He's now able to free himself up for a good part of the school holidays, and he makes full use of all the recreational opportunities in the area with his family at the weekends.

Working for you: managing your own investments, gardening, self-improvement activities such as formal or informal learning

> **Rick and Anita** have been a great business team all their married life. The business has been very successful importing and selling specialised agricultural products. The children are grown up and standing on their own feet professionally, albeit with ongoing advice from Mum and Dad. Recently Rick, who is bright and intense and who enjoys working alone, decided that he wanted much less pressure from the business. He was also concerned that almost all of their wealth was tied up in that one (precarious) business. Rick and Anita decided to sell fifty per cent of the business. Anita is still active in the business in a sales role, which she enjoys very much. Rick has decided that he will pursue his interest in investment: he manages all of their money and spends several hours a day monitoring markets, meeting with professionals and developing his own investment nous. Oh, and he now does the cooking as well! Happy My Time all round.

Part time: seasonal contracts, part-time jobs

> **Sylvie** is an experienced GP. She's divorced and happily single. She's mortgage-free and has enough invested to provide a baseline security for the future. However, she realised she had had enough of seeing patients every twenty minutes, with an ever-full waiting room looming. She knew that she had lost sight of everything else she enjoyed – her friends, opera, and her intense

interest in history. Her My Time transformation has been to establish herself as a locum: she takes contracts to relieve other GPs for holidays or sabbaticals. This allows her to manage her workload without sacrificing too much income, as she's determined to continue to work and add to her investments. And she's already written some very interesting articles on local history!

Not-for-profit (usually unpaid): charities, schools, clubs and societies

George spent most of his working career as a senior manager with a sales and marketing focus. The work was demanding: big teams, fast-paced industry, lots of travel, endless change. He knew he could take those skills anywhere and would do well as an independent consultant. He had fabulous support from his wife Helen, which allowed him to focus without much distraction on his career. The children were past their most demanding years so he could afford (financially and emotionally) to take a risk. However, one of the defining aspects of his life was his intellectually disabled brother. So, driven by a real need to make a difference, George decided to take on the running of a not-for-profit organisation that was in the doldrums. It only paid a pittance compared to his former salary, but it met all his other goals for My Time.

Family work (usually unpaid): caring for children, the elderly

Liz is single and has been prudent with her finances. She was chief financial officer and general manager for a mid-sized business in Christchurch. A qualified accountant, she was a safe pair of hands and was highly valued by the owners. As time went on Liz felt she had achieved everything that she wanted to and the business was in great shape. She knew she could easily get a GM role in a bigger business – in fact, the headhunters had already approached her. What Liz really wanted to do was move closer to her family – her aging parents needed more support, and her sister was a single parent with three small boys. She knew that moving back to Timaru would fill her life with different work – almost all of it unpaid, but very rewarding to her in other ways. She does the books for a few businesses in order to keep her hand in and to maintain some independence from her family.

Portfolio of all of the above: a little bit of them all, varying from time to time.

Work is not an 'all or nothing' thing – though you could be excused for thinking it is, in some people's careers! And it is almost impossible to run most businesses or farms without a fulltime commitment, unless your enterprise is large enough to allow professional management. Prepare for tomorrow today – always be learning the next job or preparing for the next stage.

> **Prepare for tomorrow today – always be learning the next job or preparing for the next stage**

As you plan for or adjust to your new life, consider the needs that some work might fill in your My Time life:

- Do you need to supplement income?
- What would you enjoy doing?
- What would pay well?
- How much time do you wish to devote to work?
- What are you best suited to?
- What opportunities for work do you have?
- What preparations do you need to make?

- How much structure do you like?
- How much structure do you need?
- Can you work well alone or do you need associates?

How can you use your current position to prepare for the work you want or need to do in the next stage?

What's important to you about work?

It's quite possible that you do not like your job. However, we think it's very unlikely that you dislike all aspects of work. As you are considering how you will spend your time after you give up fulltime work, it might be useful to figure out exactly what components of working are most important to you. For example, which aspects of work provide the most satisfaction to you?

Recognition.

This might include things like praise, being seen as a leader or well known in your field, earning top dollars, being influential, or having high status.

Structure.

Work can provide order for many of us. Things that are important to you might include having somewhere to go each day, having a regular schedule, knowing what needs to be done, having a plan to follow and having some predictability in your life.

Achievement.

You may get great satisfaction from things such as using your abilities, solving problems, getting things done and making a difference.

Community.

Maybe the social aspects of work give you a high.

Maybe the social aspects of work give you a high. Being on a team, feeling part of a bigger effort, being needed and useful may matter a great deal to you.

Challenge.

You may find such things as competition, winning, problem solving, learning new things and constantly changing highly motivating.

Purpose.

Providing a service, making the world a better place, responsibility or having clear goals may matter a great deal to you.

Knowing the specific things about work that matter to you should help you narrow the search for where to put your energies. Ask yourself which of these things will still be important to you in a few years' time. Some may be things you will miss only at first, when you leave fulltime work. Others will be enduring needs for you, and you may want to think about how you will replace them.

Marianne was a highly valued and very skilled intensive care nurse. It surprises her how little people understand the level of knowledge and expertise that specialist nurses have these days – not to mention the responsibilities. There was certainly no lack of challenge or purpose in her role. She wanted to make a change: her husband Ralph wasn't well and she could no longer work shifts or commit to as many hours as were needed to maintain her competencies. When she examined what she really wanted from a change of work, she realised that she regretted the way she only interacted with her patients for a short time – once they were out of intensive care she rarely saw them again. She still wanted challenge, variety and purpose in her role, but she wanted a more enduring relationship. That led her to a position as school nurse for a large private school. She oversees the health programme within the college, gets to know 'her girls' very well over the years they are at school, she has back-up cover, and she has the school holidays free. So as well as the My Time that Marianne has created for herself, she and Ralph have some great We time!

What kind of work will you do?

You won't just want any work. After all, the whole purpose of this exercise is to provide an aspect of the ideal life you wish to lead. Yes, you may need to earn a certain amount of income, but it's really important that you are doing things that you find satisfying, that give you some pleasure, and that meet as many of your needs as possible – such as giving you some stimulation and challenge.

> **As we get older, we are increasingly aware of what suits our preferences and our lifestyle.**

As we get older, we are increasingly aware of what suits our preferences and our lifestyle. It's important to make sure that the work component you have is the best fit you can get. You probably don't want more of the same:

- fulltime work, perhaps with long hours and many weekends thrown in
- being micro-managed, or even just managed

- having a lack of choice about what you do and who you do it with
- entanglement in office politics.

No doubt you can add a long list of other things you wish to avoid!

The advantages of taking control of your own 'self-deployment' (as one of our interviewees calls it) include:

Autonomy.

You are your own boss, no matter how many organisations you consult, contract or donate work to.

Direction.

You are in charge of managing your world and the sort of work you pursue.

Health.

It is very positive to be able to make your own choices about the different aspects of life that we all juggle – family, personal wellbeing, learning, work, leisure . . .

Development.

You can decide how to manage your own career, and which strengths and interests to develop.

Fun.

Choosing what you do and being fully engaged with it is fun. Why can't your work be filled with passion and fun most of the time? Identifying what's fun for you is part of the process of creating the ideal next step.

Managing your own world has many positive spinoffs, not least of which is the fact that you are in charge. You will need to think about what kind of work you want to do, how much work you want to have, and how you will arrange that in the context of the other things you will do. For example, you may have a permanent part-time arrangement with an employer; you may take seasonal fixed term contracts, leaving your summers free; or you may choose to work at just about anything, when you're not travelling overseas!

Now is a great opportunity to follow your passion. You may have spent a lifetime earning a living in work that compromised your soul; but now is a good time to work at things you really enjoy doing.

> Now is a great opportunity to follow your passion. You may have spent a lifetime earning a living in work that compromised your soul

Here are some suggestions for ways to earn an income or create meaningful work from your passions.

Food: catering; teaching cooking

Gardening: guided garden tours; helping people with their gardens; flower arranging; landscape design; flower delivery

Sport: coaching; administration; assisting with children's sport

Homemaking: running a bed and breakfast; staging homes for sale; doing a locum for people who operate homestays; finding people great places to stay/eat/visit in your locality.

Volunteering: at the local school; Victim Support; the local hospice; Save the Children, etc.

Not all of the things you love doing will be great money earners, but it's worth trying your hand at a few. You can always change your mind, or supplement the time you spend working at the things you love with some hours in paid work.

> **Bart** always champed at the bit in his role as headmaster. He enjoyed school, the kids and all of the challenges he faced on a daily basis. His whole family has always built life around the demands of his role. But school was all-encompassing and left almost no time for anything else. Even the legendary long holidays didn't help – in fact, like most of his peers he spent much of the holiday time planning, recruiting, and managing building projects and other improvements to the school. He yearned for more My Time. Bart was realistic enough to know that he had an all-or-nothing role. The only solution was to create a new career, as he felt sure he had another decade of fulltime effort left in him. He was very keen to travel (as was his wife, Elena) and had great educational contacts overseas. He used these to 'deploy' himself as a visiting lecturer in an international college in Belgium. In addition, he set himself up in business finding work placements for overseas graduates who were looking for work experience in New Zealand. And just to fill in what time was left, he embarked on a Masters degree in literature – setting himself up for the next stage of My Time.

How will you find work?

Whether you want to work or have to work, you will be in plenty of good company. Increasingly, people of 'retirement age' are returning to work, some because they must, but most because they choose to.

The secret to getting this right is to start planning for it as soon as possible. You want to find the conditions in which your talents will flourish rather than fade.

Start to do an inventory of all that you bring to the world of work. There is much more to this than updating your CV – a bald document that simply lists the roles you've held over the years, and perhaps highlights some relevant achievements; and you are probably better to redo your résumé for each role you're looking for. It may be better simply to detail the relevant experiences and competencies, rather than submit a life story – certainly so if you feel the length of your career may be seen as a negative.

It's very important that you think widely about the entire range of knowledge, skills, achievements and experiences that you can offer. Not all of these will be relevant to each piece of work or situation

> It's very important that you think widely about the entire range of knowledge, skills, achievements and experiences that you can offer

that you might approach, but it's very useful for you to have all of this information on hand. Think of it as a menu from which you can select the right mix for each potential client or employer. Consider (again!):

- what you are good at
- what others say you do/did well
- what you are proudest of
- what others praise and acknowledge you for
- what underlying abilities have allowed you to achieve
- what others think you do better than most.

It's useful to take this piece by piece and list all of the work knowledge you have. We accumulate so much over the years that we are in danger of forgetting what we know. We are also inclined to take it for granted. As a builder, for example, you will know and understand the building codes. You will also have a vast knowledge of building materials and finishes. You will know where the best subbies are in your area and what to look for. Your skills probably include building, estimating quantities, pricing constructions and managing subbies. You may well have vast experience ranging from industrial to domestic projects, big and small, and perhaps you have overseas experience. You will no doubt rate some of your work and experiences as real achievements. The message is to take stock of what you can offer and be prepared to talk about it and give examples. If you are looking to freelance as a handyman builder or to join Hire a Hubby, a full inventory of what you know, can do and have done would be very reassuring for whoever is considering employing you.

It's best to think ahead while you are still in fulltime work. Talking to your employer or colleagues can be sensitive if no one yet knows that you plan to give up your current role. However, once you are free to talk about what you hope to do next, get busy and engage others in helping you find what you want. In our experience, many employers do not want to lose good employees – at any age. You may well find that your boss is willing to accommodate you with part-time work or allow you to do some work remotely. They may be happy to have you contract back some services to them, or employ you as a consultant. You won't know if you don't have the conversation – and make it clear that you still intend to do some work. Don't be afraid to make proposals – the worst that can happen is that they say 'no'.

And while you are still in fulltime work, do everything you can to help your organisation or business to be more 'elder friendly'! Not only will this benefit all of us babyboomers, but it makes economic sense too. Demographic trends show we'll soon face shortages of skilled and experienced people – the world of work needs us!

Then, of course, there are all the other openings in your industry. You should be in a good position to see where there are unmet needs. Perhaps you have a role as a mentor or coach for juniors in your field. Maybe you would make a very good trainer, given your years of experience. Your colleagues will have close knowledge of your skills and talents, and might also offer some objective thoughts about where you could add value.

This is also the time to refresh your network, and let it be known that you are making a change and will be seeking other work. Some people find it difficult to talk about themselves or to ask for what they want. However, now is not a time for modesty or acting shy: you need as many people as possible to know that you will be available for work, and what you might be able to do for them. For a while at least, until all of this takes on a momentum of its own, you will need to get used to talking about yourself and asking for what you want – work, a referral, a contact, feedback.

> **Now is not a time for modesty or acting shy.**

Gary felt very at ease about his work search – after all he had worked for over twenty years for the same organisation and had devoted all of his work efforts to the business. He had held a senior role in finance, and everyone except Gary recognised how good he was. Because of his naturally modest personality, he hadn't grown a huge network beyond the business – Gary only ever did what was good for the business, and was largely oblivious to what was good for him! It took him some time to find his feet: he started going to the meetings of the Society of Accountants, and he attended a course on professional directing. He (reluctantly!) made contact with everyone in his network and let them know that he was officially retiring but wanted to do relevant and interesting paid work for the foreseeable future. A chance contact with a university department led him to run some short courses on finance for business owners . . . which in turn led to his first director's role. One or two more ingredients – like regular fishing trips away with his oldest grandson, and the best organic vegetable garden in Invercargill – and Gary got the recipe right for perfect My Time.

Go to work on work!

We have put quite an emphasis on the work stuff because we think it's really important to your health and happiness. We know this from all of the people we have coached and those we have interviewed for this book. No matter how much you dislike your current job and wish to be free of work altogether, you are unlikely to feel that way for long after you leave. We are picking that you are still chock-full of life and energy. The fact that you are reading this book means that you are interested in how to best arrange your life post fulltime work. No doubt you are blessed with many valuable skills and experiences. You are likely to be still eager to learn more and to continue to grow. You probably are also used to plenty of challenge and stimulation, and will miss that as soon as you have a good recuperative rest.

You will need to get your ducks in a row if you are to be successful in getting the best fit for you. To sum up a lot of what we have discussed, the ducks are:

Have a good look at yourself.

Try to get as clear as you can about what you are like and what you want. Gather as much data as you can on your skills, interests, abilities and experiences. Be as clear as you can about what you like and dislike, what's fun and what's not, what you don't want and what you do want. Try to do all of this with a flexible frame of mind – it doesn't pay to start slamming doors before they have even opened! Think about the kinds of work, workplaces and people you most want to be around. If you are thinking about working alone or for yourself, explore this a bit further if that is a new thing for you.

> It doesn't pay to start slamming doors before they have even opened!

Have a good look around.

What's out there? What are others doing? If you know people who have trod this path before you, buy them a coffee and pick their brains. Look at work that appeals to you. See what the options are for doing it in ways other than as a fulltime job. See if you can identify any gaps – what's not being done well; where businesses are suffering; what problems you could solve. Talk to as many people as possible. Note things you may need to learn and identify gaps in your repertoire that you need to fill.

> Look at work that appeals to you. See what the options are for doing it in ways other than as a fulltime job.

Start to narrow it down.

Depending on your personality, you could stay in this phase of exploration forever. At some point you have to make some choices. Be prepared to get it wrong – it's not terminal and you can withdraw and start again. More about decisions and making choices later.

Start!

At some point you have to suck it and see. If at all possible, try out some alternatives before you leave your fulltime job. You could do this in a voluntary or assistant capacity. Work experience isn't just for school kids! Use your holidays well as you approach this time. But do something – try something new, start your own business, learn something new, take on a new role, and see what works!

> **Remember to flourish, not fade!**

Being your own boss

Now there's a great idea – or is it? Many people who have been teth-ered to the corporate yoke dream of being in charge of their own work life. The lure of self-employment or owning your own business is high. It is very common in New Zealand for people, as soon as they have learned their trade, to incorporate as sole traders or freelancers, or to form a small business employing a few others.

> **Many people who have been tethered to the corporate yoke dream of being in charge of their own work life.**

Chances are that you will work for yourself in one form or another once you give away your full-time job. If you do so, then you need to think about how you are going to be a great boss for yourself. Easy, you say – you will do and expect pretty much the opposite of every manager you have had to date!

It's worth thinking about this a bit more. There are many advan-tages of working for yourself and being your own manager. They include:

■ deciding what you will or won't do

- setting your own times of work – hours, days or weeks of the year
- working from home if you choose to
- deciding what you will charge for your services
- lots of variety
- the challenge of finding and doing work on your own behalf.

. . . and you can no doubt think of even more to add to this list.

On the other hand there are some disadvantages that you may need to consider:

- Work may be uncertain and difficult to find
- You will have to market and sell yourself
- It's hard to manage the volume of work – there's usually too little or too much
- Uncertain income may be stressful
- There are no benefits such as sick leave, paid holidays or insurances
- Ensuring that you collect payment – not always easy!

You will need to think about the realities of self-employment. It takes a lot of discipline to manage your time when there are no set hours of work and no official office where you have to show up. You will also need to learn to manage 'lumpy' income – no longer will there necessarily be a steady flow of cash to your account month by month. Clients may feel they can be tardy with payments as you are a small minnow for them, and this can be very difficult, particularly if you are depending on one or two clients for cashflow. You will also need to learn to estimate and charge appropriately – it's very easy to overdeliver and undercharge. It's rare in most fulltime jobs to learn the skills of properly evaluating how much time certain tasks actually take – there's lots of 'noise' in most organisations that covers up what's actually happening. But if you are working for yourself you cannot afford to take twice as long to do things as you estimate or that you can charge for – in effect, that halves your hourly rate. We see many self-employed people who work far harder than they ever did in their previous career, but earn far less.

> We see many self-employed people who work far harder than they ever did in their previous career, but earn far less.

To make self-employment work, you need to be ready to manage yourself well, and you have to learn to be very efficient with your time. In the end, clients will pay for what you produce, not for the amount of time it takes you to do it.

Clara's husband, Neil, was determined to move to Hawke's Bay after he opted for My Time. He's continued to work as a builder but on smaller projects and without the same pressure or financial risks as before. Clara, however, had to leave her senior marketing role and decided to try to make a go of her own business. Her marketer's eye noticed how many visitors the region gets and – as a mother herself – how difficult it was for parents lugging buggies, carseats, cots and all the other paraphernalia that goes with small children. She has set herself up in business hiring out this kind of equipment through hotels, motels, apartments and guest houses, and is doing very well. Her marketing skills ensure that she has approached this professionally and that her service is exemplary. Clara and Neil are working on their skills for managing 'lumpy' income; until now they always had her regular salary. Both are thrilled – their lives are busy, but with much more My Time.

One skill away from success

If you have been in fulltime employment all your life you may find the idea of looking for work for yourself daunting. That's understandable – until now you may have just waited to be promoted within your industry on the basis of your growing competence. Perhaps you have simply brushed up your CV now and then, and gone looking for a new job when you felt you had outgrown the last one, or found yourself at a dead end. You may have responded to newspaper ads, approached a recruitment agency or even been headhunted.

Getting work for yourself – as opposed to seeking a new job – is a different thing. It pays to start thinking about work, rather than about jobs. And you may need to think about reskilling or upskilling in some areas.

Perhaps you already have many of the right attributes to be a valuable director. You might have been director of the business you have just sold, or the farm you are passing on. In that case you would be very wise to take a course in being a director, and join the Institute of Directors as soon as possible. This training is unlikely to be wasted if you have a professional background or have been a senior manager. It will also be useful if you are intending to be the director of your own new business.

Your needs may be even more specific. Many of us babyboomers are not as comfortable with technology as we might be. Depending on what kind of work you're hoping to do, you may well need better spreadsheet or PowerPoint skills, for example. If you are setting up as a consultant, it's important that you are comfortable and proficient in using all the technologies that your clients might expect. You may have been relying on a secretary to supply some of these skills in your previous role, but you will need to be able to do it for yourself now. Again, the advantage of thinking about these things early is obvious: you may be able to learn many of these things while still in your job, if you begin in time.

> Many of us babyboomers are not as comfortable with technology as we might be.

There may be particular training you should consider so that you can make the most of your previous skills and experience. For example, people who have lots of experience dealing with young people might train to be a professional driving instructor. Supervisors and managers might get great mileage out of training in coaching and mentoring – you will know and understand the context and the field of work, and may just need a bit of upskilling to make you invaluable. For example, a competent family cook might learn to present cooking classes at community colleges, thus supplementing her income as the family leaves home. Another person might use his interest in local history to build a business guiding tourists on local adventures – he can do as much or as little work as he wishes, and can dovetail this with a life of fishing, skiing and music!

It's not always obvious what you need to do to make yourself more useful or employable. It may not always be an easy or straight path. But do take heart and courage from the fact that there are many around you already doing it and thriving at it. There is great life after 'work'; in fact the best work may come after you have left your job. You are likely to end up enjoying work as never before.

The personal freedom that choosing your own work provides will give you the My Time that you have been craving. Work takes its proper place in life – a way to expend our energies and extend ourselves while giving us some income if we need it. Work fits into your life, rather than a job that takes over your life.

> The personal freedom that choosing your own work provides will give you the My Time that you have been craving.

Rally your troops

Engage everyone you can to help you figure out what you can do and find the work you want.

Try to think as broadly about this as you can. If at all possible, consider it fun and turn it into a project, for example, You Inc or Me Ltd. The more people you talk with and the more people you have contact with, the more likely you are to find what suits. We are often very poor at this, particularly if all of our 'work' has been found for us by our manager or employer. Others who have been self-employed or have run their own business will be much more used to putting out feelers and finding what they need and want.

Start with those closest to you: friends and family. Make a list of who you have, what they do and whom they are likely to know.

Consider all of the people you know through work. Unless you intend to compete directly with your employer, you will probably find that you know a great number of people who can be of help. And unless you have been horrible to those around you, you will probably find that people are willing to help and, in fact, are flattered to be asked.

Look more widely. Consider the wider social group you belong to – churches, sports teams, people your children associate with, voluntary organisations you are involved with. If there is anyone you need to meet or get advice from, the chances are you already know someone who has that contact. We live in a small country and it's not hard to get access, even to the highest in the land. In a strange but nice way, most people are happy to be asked for help, and will take a phone call or have a cup of coffee with you and – unless you make a real pest of yourself – will introduce you to others who can help.

You may or may not be good at networking in your life. Some people are oblivious – they may have been born into a large family group and never had to make the effort to cultivate friendships. Others take whatever goes with their work, but never consciously nurture these relationships. But if you wish to get much work after your official retirement, you will probably need to get good at staying in touch with your contacts. You may also need to consider how you can be a giver within your network – people are much more likely to help those who are generous with their own time and talents.

> If you wish to get much work after your official retirement, you will probably need to get good at staying in touch with your contacts.

You will get different kinds of support and contacts through different groups – they are all important. People know when they're being used, so be careful about how you treat people and be sure to thank those who take any trouble on your behalf. Give and you will receive – reciprocity is a key concept for your networking.

Me and My Time

'If you can change your mind
you can change your life.'
William James

Who might I be?

Whether you are contemplating a big change or wanting to make the most of the life you've already got, it's important to understand as much about yourself as possible.

People who don't understand themselves have a tendency to leap from project to project to job to job, and from one lifestyle to another, without much appreciation for what will really suit their unique mix of strengths, preferences and values. It's all too easy to simply copy what others are doing without enough consideration about what's right for you. We are bombarded with media stories about how others live, what they do and have, how they have made changes in their lives. All of this is interesting input, and it's a good idea to keep gathering information about the wide variety of choices and lifestyles that exist.

> It's all too easy to simply copy what others are doing

However, this is not a supermarket! Buying a new product or brand is a low-risk purchase – you can easily bin it, at little cost. But 'shopping' for a new and different way to live your life is a high-stakes decision. Changing your work or location or total lifestyle is a big investment of time and energy, and you need to make sure that what you choose is likely to be a good fit for you. The more you know and appreciate about yourself, the better the fit is likely to be.

You may already feel that you know who you are. Stop and think about that for a while. In all likelihood, you have had to wear certain hats in your work life and private life to date. You are not just who you are at work or in your private life. There are many aspects of you that may have had little or no airing, or few opportunities to showcase. This is a good time to think about all of your 'selves' and to consider which of the many aspects you want to emphasise in the next stage.

After years of living with you, if you have been paying attention you will have quite an array of ideas of what and who you are. One of the joys of aging – albeit more slowly than previous generations – is that we start to feel like we really do fit our skin. We tend to feel more comfortable with who we are, what we like, what we dislike, what we believe in, what is important for us. This said, it is often our roles that have defined us. We (the authors), for example, have learned to live in many different identities – between us we've counted at least sixteen different ones: the consultant, the psychologist, the executive coach, the author, the wife, the mother, the daughter, the sister, the auntie, the granny, the confidante, the friend, the customer, the traveller, the volunteer, the student. It is no wonder that during our busy lives we lose sight of who we are. The good news is that who we are can be understood as hardwired. It's our life experiences – the software – that continue to give us the opportunity to grow, to explore more options and more identities.

> You will have quite an array of ideas of what and who you are.

Who might you be? Well, you could spend the rest of your life lamenting who you could have been, but being a ballet dancer or a model is probably out of reach now. (But we'd be delighted to hear you prove us wrong!) Or you can look to the future and feel excitement at your options. You could be a mentor, a wise old sage, a grandparent, a gardener – the only true limitations are those you impose on yourself. And while you probably cannot be everything that you would like, you can devote your My Time to the most appealing options for you.

> **Nick** ran his own accounting practice consultancy. Len, his partner, had a senior role in education and shared his zest for work and accomplishment. Nick had been busy for decades and had first-hand experience of many of New Zealand's iconic businesses. When he came to My Time he was determined to wear as many hats as possible – after all, he had spent decades as the head bean-counter that all the clients wanted to see. In addition, he had endured all the trials of building up the practice, managing many staff and weathering several economic boom and bust periods. Now, he was determined to be a great grandfather, a mentor and friend for his grown-up kids, an active community board member and a keen participant in the arts. He's taken up the cello, and is so good at it already that he's auditioning for a string quartet.

You are never too old to have an absolutely fabulous future. You can choose to be whoever you want. It takes time and effort. By now you will certainly have learned there are no real free lunches: no pain, no train, no gain. But the good news is that you can still learn and change almost anything.

> **You are never too old to have an absolutely fabulous future.**

What are we babyboomers like?

Babyboomers have often been referred to lately as the 'me' generation. We're so lucky. We missed the two horrific world wars that wrecked the lives of so many of our parents' generation. Not only did we manage to avoid the Great Depression, we arrived as the world economy was taking off in the postwar years. We have ridden a wave of invention and wealth that has transformed daily lives – everything from affordable automobiles and household appliances to medical advances such as antibiotics and the pill. Along with material wellbeing, we have been the beneficiaries of changing attitudes – the expectations that everyone has a right to an education; that women could choose how to live their lives; and that the state would provide a social safety net.

> Of all the times in history that you might choose to live, we won Lotto.

Of all the times in history that you might choose to live, we won Lotto. On any scale, as a group we have been incredibly lucky with our time and place in history. And it continues – now our cohort is approaching what traditionally has been seen as the end of fulltime work (retirement). We are still young and mostly in very good health. We may not feel wealthy but we are indeed rich, both in material ways and in the options our lives provide.

As you'd expect, in many instances the 'me' generation is still very focused on 'me'! Our respondents talked a lot about their desire to have My Time. That's not surprising. Many feel they have been on a bit of a treadmill for the last thirty or forty years. Yes, we may be lucky and privileged in a historic sense, but most of us have worked hard for that. We are the first generation where many women worked outside the home. That was driven both by women's desire for challenge and achievement, and by our society's insatiable desire for material betterment. It had both positive and negative consequences for males and females alike – there was more money, with both genders sharing the 'breadwinner' burden; but there was also a perceived need for a proper 'stay at home' wife and mother. Once we had committed to owning bigger and brighter homes than our parents and filling them with modern appliances and cars, we were also committed to working pretty hard to fund it all. Working hours have increased over the last two decades, and with more dual-income couples it's not surprising that people are yearning for time for themselves. This does not imply that they wish to do nothing; merely that they wish to do more for themselves.

> Yes, we may be lucky and privileged in a historic sense, but most of us have worked hard for that.

Generally, we are very good at whatever we do. We have been practising it for a long time and are competent in our field. Hopefully we are still learning new things – outside our work if necessary – but doing our jobs is usually relatively easy at this stage in life. We may not be as quick as we once were, but our experience is very strong. We have lots of options to continue to enjoy some work if we want it – and if we prepare for it, as we have seen earlier.

Most of us are ready to live our lives to the full. The children are grown – and mostly behaving like adults, with the odd regression! Mortgages are usually discharged, unless we have kept upgrading our homes at every chance.

Our bodies are not what they used to be – we probably didn't appreciate what we had when we had it – and we're rapidly becoming invisible to the opposite sex. But most of us are still in reasonable shape, and still young enough to make a real difference if we make the effort.

> **Hans** had made big plans for his birthday – after all you don't turn fifty every day. The boys were choppered to the top of some rugged hills for a daring and heart-stopping downhill mountain-bike ride. Fabulous weather, fabulous terrain. All were in great spirits. Though all were of an age, all were fit and well, and living life to the full. Hans told us, however, that on top of the hill he was ambushed by a sense of the finality of fifty. He could no longer pretend to himself that time was on his side: surely now he was in the second half. Yes, he was superfit and healthy, but even so, he could hardly expect to be doing things like this for many more years. It was time to think seriously about all the other undone and underdone aspects of life – there was only so much time left, and so much left to do!

That's just a general picture of babyboomers – but what are you like?

What are you like?

It's an easy question – for other people! We all know what others are like, but so often we know so little about ourselves or how others perceive us.

So ask around. Tell people you are gathering data on yourself so as to make the best choices for your future. Ask them to tell you what they know and notice about you. What do they think you are good at? How would they describe you to others? What do they admire about you? What are your less attractive qualities?

This can be very illuminating, because it may uncover some of your 'blind spots' – things that others know about you that you are oblivious to! Some of these will be flattering – you are likely to find that others think you are very good in some areas that you take for granted. You may also be surprised to learn that others find you a challenge in some respects of which you are unaware! Remember, their perception of you is their reality of you.

Needless to say, you need to ask a reasonably wide sample of people if you are to get good data. And there is no point in asking those who might be uncomfortable telling you the truth. So cast your net widely. Here are some people you might ask:

- partner
- friends
- siblings
- parents
- peers
- manager.

Don't argue with the feedback – it will only cause your interviewee to stop talking. Just say 'thank you' for the gift they have given. Gratitude is a great skill to nurture.

> **Greg** knew he needed to make some changes. His business, though successful, was wearing him down. He had a busy graphic design consultancy with several talented – but quirky – staff working for him. All problems ultimately landed on his desk and he still held too many of the relationships with key clients. His partner, Karen, had been pressuring him for some time to get some change – before the doctor ended up ordering it. When he canvassed friends and family about what he was like, he got some surprises. He had not had a manager for two decades and no one had been giving him any feedback – or none that he heard! People were generous with Greg – if surprised to be asked, as he had hitherto seemed impervious. He learned, somewhat to his surprise, that he was perceived as a workaholic, exacting, a perfectionist and almost impossible to please, wonderful with clients but very hard to work with. At a more personal level he discovered that others saw him as close to burnout (it wasn't just a spouse's nagging, after all) and angry all the time. One person noted that he seemed deeply dissatisfied, though by all normal standards he was successful. Greg duly thanked people and took time out to process the feedback

and reflect on what it meant to him and what changes he might make.

The process and messages you receive are often not easy but they are hugely valuable.

What have you achieved?

We are not accustomed to talking about our achievements – it's not quite the 'done' thing in our culture. There's a nice humble and modest aspect to that. However, the downside is that we often remain unaware of our achievements because we don't claim them. But in the privacy of your own life or in your own notebook, it's important to have a good sense of what you have achieved. There are several reasons for this – your achievements are a signpost to:

- **What you do well.** It's unlikely that you will be claiming an achievement that does not illustrate strengths and skills that you possess.
- **What you care about.** It wouldn't be an achievement if it didn't matter. Your achievements signal what's important to you.

Think widely about your achievements. A very high achiever with a public profile recently noted that the achievement she was most proud of was nursing her mother through her final illness. It wasn't what her audience was expecting her to claim as the biggest thing in her life!

However, just like her, much of what you have achieved may be outside of your work life. Take the time to consider your proudest moments: what do they tell you about what matters to you and about who is the real you? It may make you cringe to list your achievements, but there is real insight in owning up to your 'prouds'. Go right back through your life, your childhood, your college years, your early work life, your relationships. Note what you have accomplished in all facets of your life. This is not a CV – not a list of what would impress a potential employer; rather, it is a list of the things you are happy you managed well. And you don't have to share if you don't want to!

Some things our interviewees were proud of are:

- raising children
- owning a home
- getting qualifications
- being around to help their parents
- volunteer work
- surviving separations and illness
- sticking it out through hard times
- being good neighbours
- providing for others
- doing well in their work.

And remember, we are just mining the past here for some useful information. We all have a past – some good and some not so good. There may be little in your past that you want to claim. It doesn't matter, because the future is where you are going, not the past. Your past is not your destiny. You can choose the future My Time you want.

> Your past is not your destiny. You can choose the future My Time you want.

What will you choose to achieve in your My Time?

What are you good at?

It's important to know your strengths. Generally speaking, you will be happier and more successful if you spend more of your time doing what you are good at and playing to your strengths. There is an entire industry dedicated to uncovering your strengths, and many instruments that you can use. However, discovering your strengths is not all that difficult.

Knowing what you do well is very useful when you are contemplating undertaking any paid work. Clearly you are far more likely to be useful if you are skilled at something. But it's also important to employ and enjoy your strengths as much as possible in your free time. We get a lot of satisfaction from doing things well, whether or not we get paid.

Needless to say, there are aspects of our lives and work that we are less good at. Usually they are unavoidable and must be tackled. There's no problem with that – and you can't be good at everything. However, the trick is not to sign up for something where you will be spending a lot of time or energy in areas of non-strength. It takes more time and energy, you are likely to do less well and it's less likely to be satisfying – and the outcome may be a stressed you!

Yes, you probably could work on your weaknesses – but only where they are getting in the road of you doing something you really want to, or getting an outcome that really matters to you. No amount of work on weaknesses is likely to turn them into strengths – what you should aim for is to improve enough for the weakness to no longer be a barrier to your success. So don't waste time addressing weaknesses that don't matter to you.

> **No amount of work on weaknesses is likely to turn them into strengths.**

So what are you good at? You are likely to be good at several aspects of whatever kind of work you do or were trained for. This is not a time for modesty – after all, what we are trying to do here is find the core strengths that you will base your future life on. Here's your opportunity to boast:

- What has always come relatively easily to you?
- What were you good at in school?
- What do you do better than most of the people around you?

Again, ask others who know you well.

Your strength and skills reside in you: they belong to you. They are often talked about as 'transferable skills', because they are something that go with you wherever you go. Skills you have developed and strengths you have can be used in all sorts of other contexts. Don't make the mistake of identifying too strongly with your work role – you are not your job or your work title. Think rather about what leaves work with you and the sum/package/mix of experiences, skills and talents that is you and you alone.

> **Kate** really struggled to identify her strengths. After all, she had a position description and she just did what it said – as you would! However, when she finally took the time to analyse her

skill set and to find out how others saw her strengths, she was quite surprised. In addition to the skill set she took for granted in her human resources role, she discovered that she was seen as having special strengths at establishing rapport with people, persuasion, and facilitating change. Kate had always assumed that she could only work as she did in a large organisation, probably in a main centre. She did not see how she could ever get off the treadmill of an eight-to-five day doing what she had specialised in for years. Now she began to think . . . These strengths were very portable and could be used anywhere. Perhaps she could freelance or use her skills in a different way.

What are you interested in?

There's often a great deal of overlap between strengths and interests. That's because most of us are not attracted to areas that we don't do well in or haven't much of an aptitude for. When you are considering how you will make your life more ideal, it will be important to follow your interests. You may have been lucky so far and been able to spend a lot of your life working on things that you are interested in. However, that is not true of everyone – depending on upbringing and other circumstances, many of us have spent our lives becoming very skilled in areas that we are not interested in at all!

Your leisure time may be a much better guide to what interests you. Consider how you spend free time when you are making the choices. Realistically, in many families, 'free' time is dominated by the needs and desires of others. You may have spent years of your life attending sporting events and accompanying partners and children to interests of their choosing. You may well have lost sight of what it is you really enjoy or are interested in. Ask yourself:

- What attracts you?
- What do you like to read about?

- When you do get control of the remote, what do you choose to watch?
- What have been your best holidays and why?
- What do you like doing?

Usually, people are interested in things they have skills in, and vice versa – they become good at things they find interesting. But not always. For example, many people are very skilled at aspects of their work role, such as budgeting or writing proposals, but have no interest in using these skills unless they must. Likewise, some of us are very interested in or attracted to a sporting activity, such as golf, for which we have little talent and which we would almost certainly never describe as a strength!

This is why it is important to distinguish between strengths and interests. You will want to avoid spending a lot of your time in your new life doing things that do not interest you. Likewise, where you are seeking to be paid, it is not enough to follow your bliss – you will need to be seeking work you are skilled at.

> **You will want to avoid spending a lot of your time in your new life doing things that do not interest you.**

Rowley had taught science for years. He was very competent in his field, having entered the profession with a Masters degree. Many people had wondered why he stayed in the job for so long, given that there were so many opportunities available in the field, and so much better paid. Rowley had kept up with developments in his field over the years so he was well versed in some of the scientific and medical breakthroughs that are having an impact on the quality of life for many in the Third World. He'd always regretted not progressing to a medical degree when he was younger but there were all kinds of family constraints. Rowley was seen as a great teacher but it was a skill he largely took for granted, as he didn't find it difficult to communicate and seemed to have a great talent for engaging students. When he spent some deliberate time analysing his interests he realised that his real passion was for inspiring and motivating others. In school that showed up in his converting disinterested kids to the fascination of his subject. But as he looked more widely, he realised his interest in science and solving the problems of the world's underprivileged might be pointing him to take his skills in a different direction . . .

What do you care about or value?

Values are deep-seated and fundamental to our way of seeing the world. They are enduring, and unlikely to change much over time. Whether we can honour our values in action or not may be somewhat dictated by our circumstances, but they are still likely to be very important to us.

There is a lot of dross talked about regarding values. That is not to say that values are unimportant – quite the contrary. However, the term is used very lightly. Values are often used as a corporate planning tool, but they don't translate beyond the showcase plaque into the daily actions or make-up of the organisation.

Your choices will be guided by your values, whether or not you are consciously aware of them.

True values are principles and guidelines that you live your life by. Your choices will be guided by your values, whether or not you are consciously aware of them. For example, if money and status are your key values, you will make your decisions in ways that enhance the likelihood of your realising those values. This will influence the way you work, the roles you seek, the promotions you want, where you live, what you buy, etc. Someone who values helping others, or creativity, will make quite different choices in the same circumstances.

There are values that we are supposed to cherish, and others that are less socially acceptable. However, the purpose of this exercise is not to make you popular or a poster girl/boy for any cause, but rather to help you be clear about what matters to you.

It's easy to claim that you value a very long list of things, from achievement to security to world peace. It's hard to argue that any of these are wrong, or that a sensible person wouldn't desire them. However, when the chips are down you have to choose – it's impossible to truly honour more than a few values, as you will be faced with conflicting choices all the time. So get clear on what the non-negotiables are for you. Knowing what your few core values are makes it much easier to chart a path through the myriad choices and decisions that you have about how to spend the rest of your life. When you are clear about your non-negotiables, you can make the right choices for your My Time.

When you have a clear picture of who you are and who you have been in your life so far, it's time to think about who you will choose to become as you move into My Time. We're conditioned to think we are fully formed – after all, we are all responsible adults and did our growing up decades ago, right? Not so. We're not finished developing. We grow up – and then grow up again. The best of you may still be in the future.

> We're not finished developing. We grow up – and then grow up again.

So who might you be? What might you be like?

Mel and Sue thought they had My Time all sorted. They had pretty much moved to the beach house, even though they'd kept the family home in Wellington. They were very busy being 'retired' – in fact Mel used to laugh when he said the word. He continued to be in demand trouble-shooting businesses, and he acted as a mentor for several business owners. He also had time to surf, fish, and keep up his fitness by biking. He and Sue did a big cycle trip overseas each year. They relished their freedom and felt they had it made. Then Sue's mother, who until now had been living happily and independently, began to show early signs of dementia. After some soul-searching discussions, Mel and Sue moved base back to town: Mel said that when all was said and done, he realised it was 'family first' for him. He really valued all of the other aspects of his life that they had so carefully planned and executed so well, but he knew he would not be happy unless he was true to his first value.

My Time
Health

'Life is the sum of all your choices.'
Albert Camus

Keeping you at your best

You are almost certainly going to live longer than previous generations have. That's the good news. It's not so certain you will be at your best, or even well. And there doesn't seem to be any great point in living for a long time unless you are healthy and can enjoy your My Time. Quality of life is far more important than quantity of life. So what are some of the things you need to take care of to be at your best?

Health is a really important element of happiness. You need to be physically, mentally and emotionally healthy for as long as possible. In short, you want a very long life and a very short death – not the other way around. The earlier you begin your project to be as healthy as possible the better your chances for being active and vigorous, mentally and physically, right to the end of your days. Without good health it's pretty hard to live the life of your dreams. No doubt you already know plenty of people a lot older than you who are active – walking, tramping, swimming, golfing – and who approach life vigorously – reading, thinking, debating, challenging as well as they did at any stage in their lives. You will know other people for whom everything is an effort – they are negative, do as little as possible, are uninterested in much of what's happening in the world. And many of these people may be nowhere near retirement age yet!

Start now to think about the levels of health that you would like to have in the coming years. One of the paradoxical things about health is that there is no quick fix. You have to commit to patterns of behaviour that are most likely to keep you well for as long as possible. And you can't put this off – many of us have goals for how we will live one day, when we are freed from the shackles of fulltime work. You can't afford to wait – you may well have compromised your long-term health well before then. Bite the bullet now.

> You have to commit to patterns of behaviour that are most likely to keep you well for as long as possible.

One of the ironies of life is that we often get away with very bad habits when we are younger, and so set a self-destructive pattern of overwork and under-rest, as well as lack of exercise, poor eating habits and overindulgence in substances that are bad for us. Most of us know what we need to do to be physically healthier – and there is a wealth of information available. Much of it is common sense – plenty of sleep, lots of vegetables, no smoking, not too much alcohol, and an active lifestyle.

This can all be a challenge if you are still caught up in a profession or business where overwork and self-neglect are endemic. But there's no other way to change except to start. Daily habits have the best chance of success – regular sleep times, daily exercise, proper diet. The bad stuff should be an exception – and won't do too much harm as long as you quickly revert to the new self-care rule. Once you get it firmly into your head that your current habits may be ruining your chances of ever living the good life, you will probably resolve to make changes immediately.

Goals are really important here. Do what works for you. We have noticed that people respond well to having a goal weight range, for example 65–68kg. Such a person would know that this is the weight range they need to stay in to look and feel good. Once the scales indicate that you are at the top of the range, you take action. Similarly with exercise – having a goal of walking or swimming 350 days a year keeps you on track. People often find that a bigger goal – walking the Milford Track or doing the Auckland Half Marathon or cycling around Lake Rotorua – helps to keep their daily behaviours aligned and gives them the motivation to do what they need to do each day to stay fit and active. Given that people in their eighties have done these things, there's not much excuse for the fifty- and sixty-year-olds among us!

Another worthwhile goal is to have the body and vital statistics (heart rate, blood pressure, bone density, etc) of a person a decade younger! Your doctor can do the monitoring and help you make the adjustments you need.

> **You stay young by refusing to allow yourself to get old!**

You stay young by refusing to allow yourself to get old! And more than anything, physical health staves off old age. Yes, you can be mentally and emotionally youthful even if your body is giving you lots of trouble – but it's much harder if your mobility is constrained or if you are uncomfortable or in pain.

Keith and Amy 'semi-retired' to their holiday home in Nelson. Keith still ran the family business in Christchurch from a distance, popping back regularly for face-to-face meetings. A large driver for opting for more My Time was their health. Keith had chronic back trouble and was overweight. Amy, busy with an extended family, had managed her weight well but her appearance belied the fact that she was unfit and had recently survived a brush with cancer. They were well off and financially secure for the future, but both were very aware that it wouldn't be much of a retirement if they didn't get their health under control. They sat down and did a plan – just the way they used to plan for the business. Their objective for year one was obvious, but what were the steps? They kickstarted their efforts with a fortnight at a renowned health resort in Queensland where, in addition to daily exercise, relaxation treatments and healthy food, they attended lectures on stress, nutrition and wellbeing. They each had full medicals while there and so set baseline measures for their health. On their return they got a personal trainer to work with them. New activity regimes were set and shopping and cooking habits overhauled. Both are in better shape two years later than they have been for a decade. They are looking forward to walking the Heaphy Track this year – a warm up to a sixtieth birthday trip to the Swiss Alps.

Recent studies indicate that attitude and a sense of humour are the bigger predictors of how well you age – more so than your genetics. The good news is that there is always something you can do to help you age well – have a belly laugh and a great attitude!

Get your head straight too

The brain appears to need exercise just as much as the body does. It's another case of use it or lose it. If you want to remain mentally fit and intellectually agile then you have to work at it.

The good news is that, though some physical decline is inevitable over time, there's plenty of evidence that we can continue to grow our mental capacity as we age. Far from being born with all of the brain cells you'll ever have, you can make new neurons all your life. You can improve your memory; you can learn new things; you can develop aspects of your intelligence that you may never have given any attention before. Yes, it takes more effort, but it's worth it.

The key seems to be to keep your brain active. You can do this in many ways. Continuing to work after you have retired is a great way to force yourself to remain alert and take on new things. Reading stimulating material or watching and discussing thought-provoking movies will all help. Some experts even recommend doing your usual things in new and different ways – anything to keep your mind as fit and challenged as possible.

Think about things you could do that would challenge you:

- take up a new hobby
- go on a research trip
- become an expert in an area – eg, World War I; or Yeats' poetry
- teach something – you'll have to learn it to a whole new level
- learn a language
- get a young person to tutor you in new technology
- take up chess or bridge
- maintain your own bike or car
- learn to sing
- read the *New York Times* online each day.

You get the point. Anything new you do will be better than nothing. Staying around the world of work and younger people is a great way of learning – and getting paid for it!

Keeping up with your field is worthwhile on several fronts. If you neglect the knowledge and expertise that you have taken years to acquire, it erodes, often becoming obsolete and making you less employable if you wish to work. Getting new knowledge and skills in your area is good for your mind, and hopefully it is an area that interests you, too. Staying current in your field gives you a point of contact with younger people, and makes it easier for you to remain part of professional associations – keeping your networks alive as well as stimulating you.

> If you neglect the knowledge and expertise that you have taken years to acquire, it erodes

Learning new things is good for your brain; and it makes your life much more interesting. You may well have relied on your workplace until now to decide what you needed to learn, and to provide the development opportunities. This is now your job. No matter where you live or intend to live, opportunities abound for new learning. Much of what used to be available only in cities or at universities is now available remotely and online. There are no excuses. So start thinking about what you'd like to learn . . . and take your play seriously! Your brain is the most important organ you can invest in to have the best of life.

Chris sold his tourism business a few years ago. He was exhausted from the seasonality and the uncertainty that goes with the territory. For the first year he did little but unwind. Once he'd recovered, however, he noticed how 'dull' he had become – it seemed to take all of the morning to read the paper, and he just didn't feel on top of things any more. Not good enough at fifty-five, he thought, even though he knew he would never need to work again. He'd always been interested in family history and thought he'd 'do' the family tree. A veritable library of books and research later, he's off on his third trip to Ireland and Scotland to track down the last of the clan.

Watch your language!

The most important words we use by far are the ones we tell ourselves – our self-talk. Your attitudes are fundamental to your wellbeing. Notice what you are telling yourself about the age and stage you are at – are these messages making you feel better or worse? Many of us carry unconsciously some very negative myths about aging and retirement (remember the myth busters on page 18). It's important to surface these ideas and challenge them.

> **Many of us carry unconsciously some very negative myths about aging and retirement.**

Some of the attitudes that will help your happiness over the years to come include:

Optimism.

It's too easy to focus on everything that goes wrong in later life and to assume that it is inevitable for you as well. Most of us will live and live well for decades to come. It's important to remind yourself of that, and not to be captured by all of the negativity. Stay positive.

Self-esteem.

Many of us have our self-esteem challenged in midlife. The children are grown up and no longer 'need' us on a daily basis. We may be at the end of our fulltime career and feel redundant – indeed, our job may have been made redundant. We are no longer as handsome or beautiful as we were. It's important to put the focus on what we have, can do and still are – knowledgeable, experienced, vibrant individuals. We have tons of reasons to feel good about ourselves and our place in society. Take care to nurture your self-esteem.

> **Take care to nurture your self-esteem.**

Adaptability.

Rigidity is aging – even in very young people. One of the things that helps keep us young is the ability to keep changing and adapting to our new circumstances and the world around us. Don't get stuck doing things the way you always have done – and telling everyone else so! Adaptability may relate to what we read and watch, the technology we use, where we go and what we do with our leisure, even what we eat and wear. Keep changing so that you retain a sense of belonging and don't sideline yourself.

Responsibility.

Feeling and behaving like a victim is very disempowering – and very unattractive! Take ownership of your circumstances as much as possible and continue to make all the decisions you can. Staying in control of your own affairs and the way you lead your life is important for your sense of self-regard and your optimism about the future. Stay on the front foot for as long as possible.

Humour.

Laugh whenever you can. It's great exercise and it always makes you feel better. Even the science now supports it – it really is the best medicine!

Sort your habits

Apparently four bad habits can age you twelve years! When you do the arithmetic, that's scary. So at fifty years old you are like a sixty-two year old, at sixty a seventy-two year old, and so on. Given the wealth of information we are bombarded with, you will not be surprised to hear that the four bad habits are:

1. Smoking
2. Drinking too much
3. Physical inactivity
4. Poor diet.

If you wish to do something to improve your health, it's clear what the agenda is. Smoking is difficult to kick, but all experts agree that it's both aging and very bad for you in every way.

Doing a bit better in each of the other categories looks easier. Thinking about wellness and health in terms of poor habits raises the question of which habits exactly each of us needs to address. It's always easier to replace poor habits with better ones, rather than simply trying to stop a specific behaviour.

It's the patterns of behaviour we have that undermine our health and prevent us from doing the things we need to do to. For example, many of us have good intentions about going for a walk or to the gym in the morning. However, if we go to bed too late we are too tired to get up early, and so on. Likewise, if we begin each evening with a glass or two of wine there is little chance that we are going to read something demanding or take any exercise after dinner. We are also unlikely to sleep as well as we might – and so the pattern perpetuates itself.

It's quite challenging to change our patterns of behaviour – we are used to them, they are comfortable and we probably like what we do even if we dislike the results. Think about your patterns. In what ways are you sabotaging your health, and your goals?

- Too much TV
- Going to bed too late
- Getting up too late
- Snacking
- Sitting around too much
- Driving when you could walk
- Doing no exercise in winter.

What small changes do you need to make to get better patterns operating?

Denise never paid much attention to all this health and fitness stuff – she wasn't interested and anyway she was far too busy running a cleaning agency and managing three sons who were still living at home and going to university. However, her doctor finally lost patience and said she was unlikely to be around for the grandchildren if she didn't take action. That message got through! Life wasn't going to get any simpler in a hurry so Denise resolved to make one small but significant change each month to get on a new track. So far she has made these changes:

1 Going to bed an hour earlier so she won't be so rushed in the morning, which often led to unhealthy behaviours all day long.

> **You will almost certainly live longer than previous generations – make sure you live well!**

2 Eating a healthy breakfast, which has lessened the likelihood of mid-morning sugary snacks.

3 Shopping to a list for planned healthy dinners, so that there is always good food in the house and little temptation to phone for takeaways.

4 Using a smaller plate – Denise realised she had got into the habit of thinking the portions her sons consumed were 'normal'!

5 Banning eating in front of the TV – most of her blowouts were in the evening, especially when she was watching something rather than thinking about what she was eating.

6 Going for a swim three to five days a week during lunchtime.

7 Joining a women's walking group with organised group outings at the weekends.

8 Limiting her intake of the fine wine she loves to weekends, and never more than three glasses at a time.

You will almost certainly live longer than previous generations – make sure you live well!

My Time
Money

'Money can't buy you happiness but it does bring you a more pleasant form of misery.'
Spike Milligan

My Money

It's not surprising that finances are a preoccupation of those looking at leaving fulltime work and those who have already left. First we start wondering about how long we'll live and then we worry about the cost of living too long! People deal with their concern about money in different ways. For some it's an overwhelming problem – they are consumed with worry about not having enough and are very reluctant to give up fulltime work. At the other end of the spectrum are those in denial – after all, the babyboomer generation has always been taken care of, so somehow or other 'the universe' will provide! Neither position is good: the worriers have their lives stunted by fear and they risk never getting to enjoy the best of years. The deniers are completely removed from the realities, and risk having very unpleasant shortfalls in the future because they refuse to save and prepare for when they no longer have big incomes from work. Some, through circumstances beyond their control, are unable to prepare as they intended; for example, their plans are derailed by accident, illness, redundancy or recession.

How much is enough for me?

For many there is no 'enough'. Some people hugely overestimate what they need in order to live comfortably. No amount of capital seems to give them the security they feel they need to live the life they dream of. Some of these feelings are driven by who we are: if you have always been anxious and a worrier, then you are likely to apply this trait to your finances as well. A certain amount of worry makes sense – after all, we are wired for survival. What will happen to us if the money runs out before we do? To add to our sensible fears, there is an entire industry trying to frighten us about our money in retirement. Needless to say, the advertisements you see will profess to be the answer to your every need!

> If you have always been anxious and a worrier then you are likely to apply this trait to your finances as well.

There's no easy answer to how much is enough. Enough for what? Enough for how long? What does 'enough' even mean to you?

Two scenarios:

Neville and Robyn are in their early forties. They both work in education so it goes without saying that they are not exactly rolling in money. However, with no children and a thrifty mindset, they are already mortgage-free and have a reasonable level of savings. They are now choosing to work less – just doing a bit of relief teaching and some private tuition. They reckon that the time – these precious years – is more important to them than more goods or more savings. They live frugally and reckon that they can manage very happily at this level for the longer term.

We had dinner with a group of clients a while ago. The conversation turned – as it often does among 'boomers' – to how much was enough. This, you understand, followed from the guests all talking about how busy they were and how much they longed for more My Time. Fuelled with some of Central Otago's best pinot noir, we listened as guest after guest seemed to pluck figures from the air. The range was between two and twenty [sic!] million dollars, in addition to the house!

These scenarios illustrate that the answer to what's enough is very personal – and not always rooted in any rational examination of the facts!

We end up having to find a balance somewhere between the extremes of fear and greed. We want it all – lovely homes and lifestyle and travel and expensive leisure pursuits – though we babyboomers have been very reluctant as a group to save to pay for it all. Conversely, we are afraid that the money may run out; that we may have the good/bad fortune of living too long

> **We end up having to find a balance somewhere between the extremes of fear and greed.**

to keep ourselves in the style we expect and have probably become accustomed to.

Several factors have to be taken into account to work out how much you need – or, conversely, how you can live on what you have. The kinds of things that matter include:

- How much you already have
- Where you will live
- How expensively you wish to live
- Whether you will do some paid work
- How long you think you'll live
- Whether you intend leaving anything behind.

Obviously there are a lot of trade-offs between these variables – unless you already have a lot, you may have to change your expectations about the home you will have or how lavishly you wish to live. Alternatively, while you may wish to do little or no paid work, you may need to reconsider this in the light of how expensive a lifestyle you will commit to.

Let's start with the facts (and remember the facts are friendly!)

How much do you have?

There's a very big difference between living rich and being rich. Over the last few decades most of us have hugely inflated our lifestyle. Think about the home you occupy and where it is, the car(s) you drive, the money you spend on holidays, clothing, eating out and so on. Even coffee! It's usually only when we have coffee out with our parents (who lived through poverty and the Depression) that we remind ourselves that people fed families on what it costs for a latte and a bun! Many babyboomers have a great lifestyle but very little in reserve.

> Many babyboomers have a great lifestyle but very little in reserve.

A financial planner would do a detailed net worth statement with you – how much cash would you have if you sold up everything you own? A quick estimate is more than adequate for our purposes here: you are considering how to have an absolutely fabulous life and you need a sense of what you have to start with. Tot up the value of what you own – your home (and any other property), your investments (shares, bonds, deposits), your business, any superannuation you will receive and any other major valuables. Don't bother with cars, furniture, toys, etc – they are only worth what you'd get on Trade Me, and you are probably not going to give them up anyway. Exceptions might include valuable art, classic cars, expensive jewellery, a boat you are willing to sell.

Get the total market value of your assets. Subtract any debt you have such as mortgage, personal loans, and credit card debt. The remainder is your net worth. Hopefully, you are pleasantly surprised.

Given that you must live somewhere, your home is probably not available as investment capital. Perhaps you are willing to live in a less expensive house and can release some money; you may even be intending a nomadic existence for years and can do without a house altogether. At this stage you should include it in your net worth so you have a full picture of what you have to play with.

Your net worth is what you are starting with at this point. For many people, doing this exercise is a shock. The amount of capital you have will determine how much income you can get from it. You can of course consume capital, but that will reduce the income it earns; and of course, the capital will run out at some point. Doing a net worth statement often spurs people to change their plans – or their spending. Many react by planning to work fulltime for a few more years and save most of their earnings. Others decide immediately that they must curb their spending so as to have more for future years. Either way, the net worth numbers are real and you are much better off to know how you stand. Now you know what money is available to you to invest in order to get a return that will fund your preferred lifestyle.

> Doing a net worth statement often spurs people to change their plans – or their spending.

If you have some years of fulltime work to go, it would be a great idea to plan to raise your net worth. This is the figure that really counts. Some people find it galvanising to do a net worth statement at the end of each year and to set a goal for the coming year. After all, your net worth is the sum you walk away with when you finish fulltime work. Bigger is better here!

Marcelle and Roger have every appearance of wealth. They live in a beautiful house north of Wellington, they both drive late-model European cars, the kids attend private schools and they all enjoy lovely family holidays. They are the envy of many – though most people realise that they work very hard for their high salaries in their respective professions of law and medicine. And they virtually never get a day off unless they leave the country! It was obvious why they were seeking more My Time. However, we were in for a shock. Their net worth statement revealed that they had very little: the house was still heavily mortgaged, the cars were leased and the plastic cards were maxed out from lavish leisure and entertainment spending. They were spending the lot and had been doing so for years. They were confronted with the horrible truth that income is not wealth – wealth is the bit you don't spend! The only good part of this story is that Marcelle and Roger have great earning power and can turn this situation around over the next two decades if they rein in their spending. My Time starts with them looking after themselves better so that they lessen the need to spend up big to compensate everyone in the family for their overwork.

> **Income is not wealth – wealth is the bit you don't spend!**

But how much do you spend?

Strangely enough, few people seem to have a good feel for how much it takes to run their lives. Perhaps it's not surprising. We rarely do the maths, and it takes a bit of effort. Most of us know what our gross annual pay is, but few of us work out how much we take home after all taxes are paid. Then, to confuse matters, we may be paid monthly, fortnightly or weekly. We pay some bills every few months; some monthly; and others, like groceries, on a weekly or a daily basis. Then there are the one-off costs for car repairs, house maintenance or upgrading appliances. And that's before you have to deal with both the expected and unexpected costs around family – fees, books, gifts, bailing them out of trouble, responding to pleas for cash . . . It's no wonder most of us don't have a handle on what things really cost us, or how much we actually spend. Unfortunately for many of us the short answer is that we spend everything that comes in – and sometimes even a bit more.

> **Most of us don't have a handle on what things really cost us, or how much we actually spend.**

However, if you are going to get your money in order so that you can have the My Time life, you have to get to grips with what you need to spend to live. Apologies if this is tedious but it has to be done. Start to monitor what gets spent and where it goes. You will have a great many clues on your bank statements and credit card statements. It's often the miscellaneous that's hard to track – the dollars we take in cash that just disappear on lunches, coffees, flowers, magazines, treats, the kids that keep turning up (or never leave home!). But track them you must, if you intend to continue to live as you currently do.

You are pricing your lifestyle here. It will probably shock you; but remember that the facts are friendly: you need the facts. You may be thinking that your lifestyle is about to change – perhaps you will no longer have to commute, you won't need lunch at work, or work clothes. All this may be true – but for now you are best to know where everything goes, then you can make decisions about what expenditure you need to retain and what will change.

Your current lifestyle should give you an indication for your future costs. Think about how you wish to live when you're no longer in full-time work. Try to cost this lifestyle using your current expenditure as a guide. This is how you figure out whether you have enough or whether you will need to make some adjustments to your expectations. Some people make enormous changes to lifestyle post retirement – moving location, downsizing everything, retreating from many of the activities they enjoyed. However, we notice that few drop their standard of living much – and many of the costs remain the same, or are even higher! Financial planners used to estimate that people spent only about 70 per cent of their pre-retirement income once they finished work; but patterns of behaviour have changed, as retirees nowadays are much more active and

> It's critical that you do the estimates for what your planned lifestyle will cost.

more likely to continue in much the same mode. So it's critical that you do the estimates for what your planned lifestyle will cost. Only you have any idea of how you expect to spend your time and what you are likely to spend. Costs may go down in some areas (you might decide that you can manage with one car) but may go up in others (more travel, more money on leisure pursuits). Your expenditure may drop as you age but it is unlikely to be much lower in the early years after you leave fulltime work.

Do some work to figure out what your annual costs are for groceries, entertainment and leisure, transport, travel, etc. Don't forget to allocate an annual sum for things like home maintenance, car replacement and upgrading appliances.

The purpose of this exercise is not to flagellate yourself or have a beat-up on your partner! Spending habits are a bone of contention in many households; however, you cannot plan for your future if you have no idea what it will cost you. Your capital, any other income you have, and any work you do must provide for the My Time lifestyle you want. Can you afford it? Do you need to lower your spending or do you need to plan to work some more? Your choice.

Where will you live?

This is not a trivial question when you are considering your income and costs. For obvious reasons many of us are confined to big cities and main centres for much of our fulltime careers. As much as possible, people try to live in nicer homes in nicer parts of town. All of this comes with a lot of cost, especially as most New Zealanders continue to move or upgrade their homes as their income rises.

The net effect of all this is that, for many of us, most of our net worth is tied up in our homes. No matter, you say, as you always saw having a good home as an investment. True, but you can't eat the house (though this is not quite true, as you can get a reverse annuity mortgage – but that's probably for much later in life).

The house you want to live in has a big impact on your expenditure. Put baldly, it's probably going to be the biggest factor in determining how much capital is available to give you income. Even if your strategy to grow your wealth primarily through your home was a good one (and that's debatable), the problem you now face is that unless you sell that house, your wealth is not available. Many people plan to downsize when the children are gone or the fulltime career is finished. However, few do so in any meaningful way. While they might buy a smaller townhouse in the same city, or move to another part of the country, people are very reluctant to take a drop in housing standard – so the smaller townhouse with a handkerchief lawn costs as much as you got for the sprawling family home on a quarter acre or more!

Just as with every other aspect of lifestyle, we inflate our expectations of housing standards. And many people are not ready to give up all of the amenities of the lovely family home with its carefully tended garden, etc. Besides, where will family, friends and the grandchildren stay when they visit?

But right now, you are probably looking at a net worth statement where nearly all the worth is in the house. What to do? Think hard about the trade-offs. You can sell and move to somewhere much smaller or cheaper. This may mean moving to a less attractive suburb, or moving away to a much cheaper part of the country – but at least you will then have far more money to spend on other things. Alternatively, you can decide that you will lower your living expenses significantly, or settle for far fewer trips in New Zealand or overseas. Another option is to do more paid work or to stay in your fulltime role for a few years longer.

People solve this problem in many ways. Some decide to rent. Others relocate to the bach or boat, or take up an itinerant life overseas with a view to making a decision much later. The home can be sold or rented out in the interim. Moving to an attractive place on the coast, or to Queenstown, is likely to be just as expensive as where you are. There's no point in moving to a small town in the hinterland where house prices are cheaper, if you are going to fly around the country frequently to see family and friends – you have just transferred budget from one line to another.

A good place to start is to list what you see as your options, and cost them out.

The work question – again!

We have already made a strong case for continuing to work after your fulltime career – we think the advantages are obvious on many fronts. Not least of these is that you can earn some income. The income you can earn or the amount of work you may wish to do can seem trivial compared to what you commanded when you were working fulltime; however, we can't stress too much the difference even a relatively small amount of supplementary income can make to your finances.

Every dollar you earn is a dollar you don't have to earn from your investments or a dollar of your capital that you do not erode. Unless you have quite an amount of capital, you are probably already feeling nervous about funding your future lifestyle from savings alone. You have the option of bridging the gap between your expected returns from investment and your lifestyle by continuing to earn some income.

We have already traversed the many options you have to continue to work. In the light of your identified need of extra income, you may want to revisit those chapters and think again about what you can do and how much you are prepared to work. It pays to be both hard-headed and realistic about this:

Timeframes.

You may well feel at the moment that you will want to do some work forever. That, of course, is with the optimism and energy of the fifties; you may not feel the same in twenty years' time. There is always the (remote) possibility that no one will want to pay us in our eighties! We simply don't know. There are trends towards hiring older workers (who are seen as more reliable and with better people skills) but who's to say what will prevail a few decades from now.

Suitable work and work skills.

Some skills are easier to apply to earning income – for example, professional expertise that can be deployed in consultancy or contract work. Other skills become less marketable; for example, it can be difficult to carry out many of the trades as you age, because the work is physically demanding. There has to be a market for what you do outside of fulltime work or specialised organisations – much of the sales and marketing work that people do in large organisations (for example, banks) is difficult to apply at the level of self-employment or part-time jobs. You may have to upskill or reinvent yourself. Staying current and in touch are key, too.

> There has to be a market for what you do outside of fulltime work or specialised organisations.

Health.

You may be hanging out to reduce the overwork, stress and general self-abuse of your career. Your health may already be compromised, and you may not feel you can take on too much. Over time, your ability to work also becomes less certain. It's hard to be sure that you will be fit to work for decades to come. This is not being pessimistic, but rather ensuring that you do not start to live (and spend) as if you were going to have income from work for many years to come.

Think about the work component of your future life from a financial perspective. Estimate what you think you can earn over the coming years, and do your rough figures again with this in mind. Best to keep working in pencil with an eraser at hand!

> **Think about the work component of your future life from a financial perspective.**

Great expectations

There may be other income that you can reliably expect to have. We approach this area with some caution as it's hard to have much certainty about the future – the more so the further ahead you look. As we write, all Kiwis expect to receive New Zealand Superannuation. This is taxed, but it is not means tested. Depending on your expected level of lifestyle, it represents a great foundation or provides a few extra luxuries. It's hard to predict what the future holds: governments all over the world are grappling with pension costs, and the number of younger, taxable workers who can fund them seems to be diminishing. But the closer you are to super age the more certain this income is, for the near future at least.

On the other hand, the younger you are the more time you have to accumulate funds through KiwiSaver. Time matters, of course, but no matter how close to retirement you are, this is still worth doing because the returns on your own contributions are very high. However, the real sums are likely to be low unless you have many years to contribute.

Many of our generation are likely to inherit quite an amount of money. One of the greatest transfers of wealth in history is about to happen as the generation ahead of us sells up property and other assets, and babyboomers succeed to this wealth. You may be lucky – or not! It never pays to count on legacies, and it shouldn't be your only strategy as you never know what will emerge – trust issues, other relatives, unforeseen commitments, etc. You can never be sure until the money goes into your account. However, many babyboomers will have great expectations of being cared for by the inheritances they receive.

> **Many of our generation are likely to inherit quite an amount of money.**

So, how much income you expect to have is likely to be a combination of several factors:

- NZ Super (on reaching 65)
- KiwiSaver (on reaching 65)
- Income from your investments
- Income from any work you do
- Income you might receive from legacies or trusts.

How long will you need it for?

If you arrange your financial affairs perfectly you would go out on the last dollar – you could spend it all because you could be sure to die just as the money ran out! That's not so easy to organise, however. The real issue here is making an estimate of how long you will live – or rather, how many more years your money must last.

Planning for the rest of life was relatively easy when people only lived for a few years after they finished their job – the time period was short, you didn't need so much capital, and inflation wasn't much of an issue. However, as we have pointed out before, you may well be looking at up to another fifty years of life. It doesn't matter if you have oodles of capital – it will keep on earning income. However, if you are planning to spend capital – eat into your investments or 'eat the house' – then it matters a lot. You risk consuming it all and still living for years after.

> People are sensitive about discussing or even thinking about their likely lifespan; however, this is not an issue that can be ignored.

People are sensitive about discussing or even

thinking about their likely lifespan; however, this is not an issue that can be ignored. There's a big difference between expecting to live for another twenty years, and expecting to live another thirty or even forty or fifty! Over the last century we've added nearly thirty years to life expectancies in the Western world. And while life expectancy figures are a guide, they are only averages. The percentage of centenarians in the population is the fastest growing group – which is food for thought.

It makes good sense to live each day as if it were your last (appreciate and enjoy every minute) – but also to live each day as if you will live forever. That implies prudence at every turn – looking after yourself as if you were to inhabit that body for decades to come but also watching your spending as if your money has to last for a very long time. And it may. The younger you are now the more likely you will live to a very old age – all things going well, you still have time to take the optimum route regarding your health, and you will also likely benefit from the many breakthroughs in medical science.

> It makes good sense to be very conservative about your predictions for your money.

So it makes good sense to be very conservative about your predictions for your money – ie, err on the side of assuming a long life. The more you expect to eat into your capital, the more this applies.

Where should your money be?

This is a very specialised area and really beyond the scope of this book. That said, there are some general principles you should keep in mind when you visit a professional (not a commission salesperson!) for individually tailored advice.

Risk.

Assuming you are approaching or already in the second half of life, your first priority must be to avoid losing what money you have. This sounds obvious, but do reflect on the horror stories we have all become accustomed to hearing over the last few years of people who put all of their money in finance companies or mortgaged the house to invest in 'blue chip' apartment developments. Having all your eggs in one basket such as a farm, a business, geared residential property or shares is a great way to create wealth, but it's not so clever when your primary focus is to preserve wealth. The whole area of risk is a fascinating one – as long as it's not your own money that's been lost. Different personalities have different risk tolerances. However, irrespective of how you feel, your biggest risk when you enter the second half of life is that you lack the time to rebuild your wealth if you lose what you have. It's always tragic to have your wealth decimated – but much more so if you are in your fifties and beyond. So think carefully about the downside as well as the upside, whatever your personal attitude to risk. Keep asking what if – and if the answer is horrible, be very careful with your investments.

Ultraconservatism.

After that you might be tempted to put your money under the bed or leave it all in the bank. Unfortunately that's too risky as well. The house might burn down, you might be burgled or the ants may eat it if you keep it to hand. The bank is pretty safe, but inflation will erode the value of your funds – and it simply won't earn enough (unless you have squillions) to keep you in the style you no doubt want over the longer term. If you were expecting to live for relatively few years, keeping the money in the bank or in bonds would probably work; but

> The bank is pretty safe, but inflation will erode the value of your funds.

if you are going to live for decades you will need some growth as well, and you won't get it here. The value of your capital sum will be worth less each year. You only have to look back a few decades to compare what $100,000 bought then and what it buys now.

Growth.

So at least some of your money must be invested in growth assets – things that will rise in value at least in line with inflation. This means that some of your investment will need to be in businesses and property. You don't need to do this directly – and you probably shouldn't, unless you have demonstrated particular skills in these areas. Having significant amounts of money tied up in a single business or property becomes more risky as years advance – you are safer to spread your bets across many businesses and properties. There are several ways of doing this – and you should seek professional advice.

Diversification.

Spreading your investment in growth assets across a range of quality businesses and properties is one way to diversify. You will need to consider several other methods of diversification. As New Zealand is a very small economy you would be wise to have a significant portion of your wealth offshore – the economy is too fragile to risk having all your wealth here. A farm or other business in New Zealand may have made you wealthy; but that is no way to preserve your wealth. Human nature being what it is, we tend to feel that what we know and what is close is less risky – but that is not the case. Consider what foot and mouth disease or a major terrorist attack quite close (Australia, say) would do to your wealth in New Zealand – property prices might collapse; tourists might stop coming, which would take out several businesses; the dollar might become play money . . . It's also important to diversify your wealth across asset classes – a fancy way of saying that you need some of your money in business, some in property, some in bonds and some in deposits. How you allocate the proportions will largely determine the returns you receive over time. Diversification is all about spreading your bets – you don't want to be in a situation where all your fortunes are linked so that anything that affects one aspect of your wealth is likely to affect all others as well. We have recently seen how tragic it has been for many people who had 'diversified' their savings across several finance companies. There was in truth no real diversification here, and the conditions that toppled one led to several more failures taking out all their wealth.

> Diversification is all about spreading your bets.

Timing.

Many people have lump sums to invest at the point of finishing full-time work. You may be collecting all your superannuation, selling a business or farm, or selling the bach or family home. One of the traps of having a lump sum to invest is that even with good professional advice regarding asset allocation, you are vulnerable to the timing of the investment. If all of your money goes into the markets over a short period of time (shares are purchased; property bought, perhaps through listed property trusts; bonds selected; term deposits set) you may have chosen a good time (bottom of the cycle) or a poor time (top of the cycle) – there is no way of knowing. We know where the markets have been, but not where they are headed. Again, beware of commission salespeople who only get paid when you purchase. The solution to this problem is to drip-feed your investments into the markets – that way you take the timing risk away (the fancy name for this is 'dollar cost averaging' – go figure!).

Keeping your portfolio balanced.

No matter what way you allocate your assets – for example 50 per cent to growth assets and 50 per cent to debt assets – the proportions will be lost over time as the assets change in value. For example, if you have 25 per cent of your portfolio in property, and property values surge, it is quite likely that you will find that property now accounts for more than one quarter of your asset allocation. Unwittingly, you can end up with an asset allocation that might be quite wrong for you if you do not keep an eye on values. It's probably best to choose a date each year (like your birthday) to review your portfolio and ensure that it is still likely to give you the best balance between the risk you can take and the returns that you want.

> Unwittingly, you can end up with an asset allocation that might be quite wrong for you if you do not keep an eye on values.

The money risks we face

Life is risky. There are no guarantees. We should have some sense of that by this stage. It doesn't pay to dwell too much on the downside as that can make for a joyless existence – and it's hard to have an absolutely fabulous time if you are always worried. However, our blissful and long-awaited My Time is likely to be derailed unless we have some level of vigilance about the real risks we face.

> Our blissful and long-awaited My Time is likely to be derailed unless we have some level of vigilance about the real risks we face.

The sensible approach to risk is to acknowledge what's likely and to take appropriate action if the consequences look serious. In the first half of life the major financial risk our families face is that we die too young or become unable to earn. Most people quite sensibly mitigate these risks by carrying life insurance (at least until the mortgage is paid off) and having disability cover so that there is either a lump sum or an income stream to tide the family over such an eventuality.

The financial risks you face when you give up fulltime work are different. It does not pay to obsess about them, but they need to be on your radar. Some of the things to be mindful of include:

Inflation.

Inflation is the borrower's friend, as many of us found out when we took on what seemed like huge mortgages many decades ago. Some of us paid huge interest rates when inflation was galloping away in the 1980s. It worked for us because our houses went up in value, while the real cost of our mortgages looked quite small after a few years; and of course our salaries were growing with inflation (not to mention our own stellar achievements!). What we forget is that the same period wiped out the savings of older people who had all their money in Post Office Savings accounts at fixed interest rates. Their incomes didn't go up – and at the same time the real value of their capital sum diminished. We have got used to quite low levels of inflation in the interim, and we don't hear so much about it now. However, even quite a low level of inflation (2–3 per cent) matters a lot if you are looking at twenty, thirty or even forty years. And it's always possible that inflation could get away at higher levels again. We do need to stay alert to this. As before, one of the best antidotes is to keep a proportion of your money in assets that will appreciate with inflation – businesses and property, or shares in the same.

Poor asset allocation.

We mentioned earlier that the way you divvy up your investments between business/shares, property/shares in listed property trusts, bonds and deposits/cash largely determines your returns. Generally speaking you can expect higher returns from the growth assets (business and property), though you will have less certainty about the returns (volatility). But if you play for certainty (bonds and deposits) while you will know what income you will earn, you may miss out on both income growth and capital growth. That might not matter too much over the short term but it will make a big difference over decades. With previous generations, financial planners commonly put all of a retiree's savings into bonds and deposits, as it was safe and income flows were assured. However, because we are inclined to retire earlier and live for much longer, that strategy has real risks for babyboomers. To mitigate this risk, you need to allocate enough to growth assets. As a subset of this, you will need to continually rebalance your portfolio – for example, you might decide to have 50 per cent allocated to equity assets (business/shares and property/shares in listed property trusts) and 50 per cent to debt assets (bonds and deposits). However, within a few years that could have become 70/30 per cent, with changes in asset values. You will need to keep an eye on your investments to ensure you do not inadvertently become over- or underweighted in your allocations. For the long term, your risk is that you do not have enough in growth/equity assets.

> You will need to keep an eye on your investments to ensure you do not inadvertently become over- or underweighted in your allocations.

Living too long.

Ironically, just as one of the big financial risks earlier in life is dying too young, living for far longer than you expect is a risk for babyboomers. As you can see, there is considerable overlap in all of these areas. However, the point is that we do need to think longer term. Humans are not good at this. We have great difficulty imagining what our life will be like more than a few years hence. We are so consumed with our present circumstances and what we want in the immediate future that we tend to ignore the longer term: witness our profligacy over the last few decades in terms of lifestyle, and our refusal to save even a pittance from our pay packets over thirty-year-plus careers. We got away with it thanks to economic growth, and the fact that our incomes kept rising and credit was easy. That won't work for us post fulltime work. If we want the rest of life on our terms, we have to plan to make our money last.

Rising healthcare costs.

This is a biggie. There are several factors involved. We expect better care than ever before. Healthcare costs are growing well in excess of inflation – partly due to new technologies and largely, we suspect, due to poor management in the health sector. The facts are that the public system is overwhelmed, and the cost of insurance premiums for over fifties is high and rising. There needs to be a bit of fat in your planning to pay for treatments that you may not be covered for. If you don't buy the argument for taking care of yourself in order to have an absolutely fabulous time, then at least consider the economic argument – you can't afford to be unhealthy! It simply costs too much. So off the couch and on yer bike!

Spending too much.

It should be clear by now that you can't take the risk of spending too much in the early years after giving up fulltime work. There's a balance here – people want to do the big My Time things like going on that OE they've put off for decades, buying a sailboat or climbing Mt Kilimanjaro. And you'd be silly to deny yourself your heart's dream – after all, having an absolutely fabulous life is what this book's about.

However, beware of blowouts. You really can't afford to erode capital much at this point – you will be eating the goose that's supposed to be laying eggs for the next few decades. Delay spending any capital for as long as possible (and, as mentioned before, the easiest way is probably to focus on still earning some income). Beware of the kinds of well intended impulsive spending we see – for example, the urge to pay for a dream wedding, or fund one of your children into a home or business. You might feel moved to pay off a student loan or other debts for someone else, or lend significant unsecured money to family. It's easy to see why you might do this, but the effect on your wealth may be disastrous – and you are serving no one by making yourself poor and dependent for the next several decades. Not being a drag on your family in the years to come is one of the best gifts you can give them. And if there's anything left when you're gone, that's a bonus. Be very wary of impoverishing yourself at this stage of life – you can't recover, and the effects on everyone you care about and who cares about you are enormous.

> Not being a drag on your family in the years to come is one of the best gifts you can give them.

Live below your means

We're guessing that you feel it's most important that you can live your life in security and comfort. Obviously, it's best to be conservative with your spending so that you leave a margin for error in your calculations: your investments don't do as well as you hoped; you have unexpected costs (family problems, ill health, etc); or you live much longer than you expect!

Always be mindful of what really matters to you, and don't spend money that doesn't give you real value. In other words, this is all about priorities. Most of us have waited a very long time to be able to do what we want, when we want, where we want, with those we want to be with. It is your means that allow you to make these choices. This is really precious My Time, and should not be squandered by spending money on things we value less or not at all.

> Always be mindful of what really matters to you, and don't spend money that doesn't give you real value.

That may represent a real change of outlook for our generation. Our parents' generation always undergeared their lives – they never lost their sense of dread about the Depression, the austerity after the war, the periods of high unemployment, and low levels of state support.

Conversely, the babyboomer generation was overleveraged – we often wanted everything, and well before we had earned the money to pay for it. This only works as long as the high incomes keep flowing – and the end of fulltime work is the end of that for most of us.

This may mean tough decisions in some families. One that we see frequently is the dilemma over tertiary education costs. Many parents feel that their children should not be burdened with a student loan. This is often because the baby-boomer generation got their education for free. However, paying for tertiary education up front is a very big hit for many who are about to, or have already, given up fulltime work. It's a huge drain on

> **The babyboomer generation was overleveraged**

capital that will be needed to fund the next few decades. The student, on the other hand, can take out an interest-free loan and has at least forty years of income-earning years to repay it. It simply doesn't make sense for parents to fund this unless they have a significant surplus of wealth.

It will be counterintuitive for many of us, but keeping our spending well within our expected income levels is one of the best ways to enjoy the My Time we yearn for. It would be a shame to spoil it with worrying about how we're going to pay for it!

It should go without saying, but it's really important to get rid of debt if you still carry any. Some people may have mortgages – perhaps they have moved to a better home recently, or started a new relationship. Others may have taken out personal loans for major renovations or purchases. Still others have lots of debt on credit cards . . .

> **It should go without saying, but it's really important to get rid of debt if you still carry any.**

Servicing debt is a big draw on your income once you are no longer working fulltime. Make every effort to discharge debt as soon as possible, and agree that you will never incur any more.

Borrowing to invest is risky. It makes sense when you are young, as the leverage makes a big difference when you wish to buy a business or farm, or want to be an aggressive investor in property or shares. However your potential losses are geared as well, should your investments fail. It's too risky to have much debt when you are no longer working fulltime and lack the time to recover your losses. Geared investments should be a young person's game.

And enough is enough!

You may well have lost the will to live after reading all this about your finances! However, even though you cannot ignore the money, it's important not to allow that to become the main preoccupation. How much do you really need in order to afford most of the elements of life as you want it?

We are conditioned to believe that more money will make us happy and satisfy our desires. The body of evidence (and happiness has been a fashionable area of research lately) is against those beliefs. Once our basic needs are met, further happiness and satisfaction are largely about other things, such as having a sense of purpose, good relationships with family and close friends and a sense of connection to our world.

So it's important not to get sidetracked by money when you want to build great My Time. Be as clear as you can about what is really important to you. If you cannot get everything that you want, make sure that you concentrate on the aspects that are most important to you. It's important that we don't set the bar too high for material goods – many of the things

> If you cannot get everything that you want, make sure that you concentrate on the aspects that are most important to you.

that we consider essentials today were luxuries until only very recently. Media such as TV and the internet have made us acutely aware of the lifestyles of the rich and famous, and unwittingly we compare ourselves to them. However, no amount of income will ever be enough if you insist on having it all.

> And there's a real downside to having too much: you'll lose your focus on what really matters to you.

And there's a real downside to having too much: you'll lose your focus on what really matters to you. You'll spend a great deal of your precious life looking after stuff – houses, cars, equipment. You could end up serving all this stuff in your life rather than having, doing and being what you really desire in your life. And your life after work should not be about worry and stress and care, but about having the time and freedom to really enjoy your time – My Time.

Here are some scenarios and recommended actions. Which one fits your situation?

> You have done all the suggested work about your net worth and the cost of your hoped-for lifestyle and found that there is a major gap. Despite your best efforts to trim your expectations and take account of all likely sources of income, there's still a major shortfall.

Recommendation: Get as much paid work as you can, and save as much as you can as fast as you can.

> Your calculations show that you can afford to have most of the lifestyle you want. You think you could get by on what you have. However, there are some additional things you'd like to do or have, such as some big overseas trips in the next decade.

Recommendation: Seek some work, and budget that income for extras like travel.

> Your numbers are sweet! There will be no shortfall unless you allow your spending to get out of control or you suffer a major calamity. You can do pretty well whatever you like with your time. You do have some concerns about being 'idle' after so many demanding and fulfilling years of work.

Recommendation: Consider some not-for-profit work such as mentoring, directing a charity – or start a new business, just for the hell of it!

My Time
Love

'Love is friendship set on fire.'
Jeremy Taylor

The VIPs in your My Time

As you contemplate or go through a major transition such as giving up fulltime work, it's important to keep the communication channels open with the Very Important People in your life. It's not uncommon for people to do a great deal of thinking and planning about what they want and dream of – and then spring it on family as a fully formed idea. This does not usually land very well, unsurprisingly!

It goes without saying that the earlier in life you begin to think and talk about these sorts of changes, the better. Include your partner in these stages as much as possible. For example, the earlier discussion about dreaming and visioning for the future is the sort of exercise that two can play very well – considering the issues individually, and then sharing ideas and wishes. Clearly, it's better for everyone if you are more or less on the same page from the start. This avoids the kind of situation where one person is planning to spend most of the rest of their life fishing and hunting, while the other is planning to indulge their passion for art by touring the great cities of the world! And it's not just the big decisions, like where to live; one or both of you finishing fulltime work will test just about every aspect of your relationship. Many aspects of your life will be up for discussion and renegotiation – especially how you spend time, energy and money. It's also quite normal for each of you to be at a different stage – with one of you ready and eager to give up fulltime work and the other not so sure.

The need to fund how you want to live highlights the need for discussion and compromise. Very few families have the wherewithal to do all of the things that everyone wants, so the earlier you negotiate some of these trade-offs, the better. Some of the things that need to be discussed include what parents will and will not fund. For example, children may be taking it for granted that they can continue their education almost indefinitely, live at home and have fees and books funded by their family. This may not be possible for you; and you need to have that conversation. It's possible that you want (or need) adult children living with you to pay board, so you can quit fulltime work. You shouldn't feel bad about that – after all, your children have had a good start in life and are now adult and must take responsibility for themselves.

Similarly, when you and your partner have discussed your finances, you may need to be clear with children about their expectations for the future. It's likely that you cannot plan to leave legacies to them or their children, and you may want to make this explicit.

You may also be looking after your own parents – perhaps they are living with you, or are dependent on you in a number of ways. For the same reasons, make sure that you understand their financial circumstances. It's not uncommon for people to have to shelve their own plans because they find out – too late – about the unhappy finances of their parents. You may need to check that wills have been made and

168

are up to date, enduring powers of attorney are in place (for financial affairs and for care) and family trusts are being properly managed.

It's not for nothing that we are described as the sandwich generation. We are sandwiched between the younger generation, who seem to take ever longer to become independent, and our parents' generation, who are often reliant on us for care and comfort. And you do have to talk to all layers of the sandwich and try to keep the lines of communication clear. It's much better if everyone has a shared understanding of the picture, your long-term plans, and what they can expect to happen. So make sure that you:

- Start these conversations as early as possible
- Say clearly what you want to happen
- Don't make assumptions about what others want
- Ask about others' wants and expectations
- Talk about the finances, as appropriate.

For better or worse

We may have a lot of adjusting to do after we leave fulltime work. While many women may be used to oscillating between periods of work and periods of time spent in the home, it's a new experience for most men. After the initial flurry of activity – domestic chores, tidying the garden or the garage, a bit of repairs and maintenance about the place – it's not uncommon to find men spending rather a lot of time about the house. Women often complain of this, especially if he doesn't have enough work to do, or other activities that take him out of the home. He's bored; she's irritated. Wives who have been used to having the home to themselves can feel very aggrieved at having their space invaded.

> It's important to set up work areas if you are planning to work from home.

On the subject of space, it's important to set up work areas if you are planning to work from home. It's very annoying and very distracting for everyone else if you commandeer the kitchen table and have work strewn throughout the home. You will also need to work out new routines, and be sensitive to each other's needs. As one interviewee said, she married him for better or worse – but not for lunch! Perhaps you'll agree that lunch together is a·

nice habit and adopt it easily, but it pays to be wary: if your partner has a different routine they may wish to leave things as they are. Partners who have been fulltime at home may already have their days filled, and the last thing they want is to be tied to being at home at midday.

If you are both leaving fulltime work at the same time, or moving to a new location to begin a new life, it may be simple to mesh your new routines. However, be wary if the other person is already established in their pattern – your expectations of having the world revolve around you may not be welcome!

Your relationship, if you are in one, matters. But relationships are rarely static. They get better or worse. They are, to some extent, renegotiated every day. When one of you is making a big transition such as giving up fulltime work there will be a major renegotiation – whether you do so consciously or not! A big change like this highlights the state of the relationship: a good one is likely to get stronger, whereas a poor relationship may show signs of increased tensions. There could be additional stress if one partner is ceasing fulltime work unwillingly – because of illness or redundancy, or simply to be available for their partner.

> Relationships are rarely static. They get better or worse.

You may also be at different stages in your own development, with one of you seeking more ease and fewer commitments while the other is eager to dive into new experiences and challenges. It takes quite a bit of talking and mutual appreciation and tolerance to work out how you will best accommodate each other's wishes and plans.

Think of it as a 'job' issue – there's a major change afoot and you may both need new job descriptions! That may help to depersonalise some of the issues and allow you to focus on your respective roles. Who will be responsible for what aspects of your lives? It's not unusual for couples to have had very clear and divided responsibilities – for example, she may have earned most of the money and he may have taken most of the responsibility for the children's education. Now that period is probably over. Who is responsible for what? Who must be consulted on which issues? How will you share chores and space and accountability for your lives together? Think of all aspects of your My Time, such as investment, banking and bill paying, gardening, maintenance, entertainment, fun, travel, housework, shopping and food.

Revitalising your relationship

The years of building a career and raising a family are very challenging for most couples. Depending on the demands you face, you may end up leading almost separate lives. One partner may have been away from home a lot, working long hours and perhaps travelling a great deal, while the other has been frantically busy keeping the show on the road, dealing with schoolwork, ferrying children around and filling in for the largely absent parent. These roles used to be gender-stereotyped, but less so in recent years. You may both be frantically busy in your careers and juggling family concerns, with a flotilla of hired help to manage as well. Whatever the scenario, you may have spent little time together for years, other than checking in with each other.

> You may have spent little time together for years, other than checking in with each other.

All this changes as time passes. The kids become less dependent and usually want to see your car or credit card more than you! Eventually they 'sort of' grow up and leave home for longer and longer periods – though we have all got used to them boomeranging back at the first sign of trouble!

Anyway, when things quieten down and we start to contemplate finishing fulltime work, the quality of the relationship comes to the fore again. Many of us need to spend time reinvigorating that relationship – she is not just 'Mum' and he is no longer just the 'main breadwinner' or wearing the 'Dad' hat. Our future happiness depends on this primary relationship working well. You are going to see a lot more of this person, and it's important that you enjoy each other's company – all the more so if you intend to travel together or move to a new location where you will be more dependent on each other.

It's time to rediscover shared interests or begin a new hobby or learning project together. One of the best things about ceasing fulltime work is that it allows you to spend some more time together. On the other hand, don't overdo the togetherness – this may not go down well with your partner. This is a great time for each of you to pursue your own interests; and at the same time, to be respectful of the things your partner wants to do and the people they want to spend time with.

> It's time to rediscover shared interests or begin a new hobby or learning project together.

Loneliness is a very hard road to travel. A good relationship is well worth the effort it takes to nurture.

Who do you want
to be around?

One of the traps of relinquishing fulltime work is that you can inadvertently narrow the range of people you are in contact with. It's not uncommon for people to end up seeing and socialising only with people like themselves. Be mindful of restricting and narrowing the contacts you have. In fact, one of the better arguments for continuing in some form of work is the connection that it provides with a range of age groups, social classes and points of view. It's all too easy to become rigid in your thinking and outlook because you have little or no interaction with younger people, or people with different experiences and backgrounds.

Just as you may well be spring-cleaning all areas of your life with a view to making big changes in how and where you live, now is a good time to review the social and network aspects of your life. Given who you wish to become and how you wish to live your life from here, have a good think about how you spend your social time, and which

> Have a good think about how you spend your social time, and which networks you wish to belong to.

networks you wish to belong to. For example, it will be difficult if you are making big changes to the way you want to live if you continue to associate only with the same folk you have always socialised with. Be wary of people we would describe as toxic – those who will encourage you to play small, and will pour cold water on your dreams and plans. Some people are scared of others making significant changes, taking new risks, exploring new avenues and demonstrating lots of energy. Their impulse will be to pull you back into line, so that they can remain in their comfort zone. Beware of allowing others to curb your enthusiasm – these people are dream stealers! It would be unkind and unnecessary to 'drop' members of your extended family and friends who are unlikely to be supportive of your plans for a fabulous life; but be conscious that you may well experience some efforts to undermine you. It pays to be wary of who you allow to have space in your life.

Give some thought to the new groups and friendships that you may want to develop. You are likely to make big shifts in how you allocate your time now that you will have much more My Time. Who do you want to be around? What kinds of people do you want to spend more time with? How will you find like-minded and supportive groups for leisure activities, shared interests and socialising?

Keep making new friends of all ages. One of the traps of committing to a fulltime career is that our work colleagues are often our social group by default – we don't have time for anything else! Much of this disappears once you leave the fulltime role; so be conscious of the need to cultivate new friendships and great relationships. This isn't simply about shared hobbies or similar social class – it's about finding good people whom you can befriend and who will be there for you over the long term. This time of life is also one where it is wise to mend damaged family ties and reinvigorate past friendships that have been suffering or have lapsed from neglect.

Nurturing your clan

'Network' usually implies relationships that are based on work. Your network is very important, especially if you wish to continue to do some work. But at a personal level, your family, clan, rellies, extended whanau – whatever you like to call them – are essential to your ongoing wellbeing and happiness. Give them the care and attention they deserve.

> Your family, clan, rellies, extended whanau – whatever you like to call them – are essential to your ongoing wellbeing and happiness.

One of the downsides of the 'building' years in our lives is that we are so busy, we can be unwittingly neglectful of these relationships. It takes all our energies to go to work, manage the week and keep the show on the road. But beyond our immediate, often nuclear family, we all belong to much bigger tribal groups – parents and other elders, cousins, inlaws, neighbours, children's friends, blended families, childhood friends, etc. There are times when we have all been rueful about some of these relationships. But overall, this wider group is very much part of who we are – and it is a precious thing. One of the advantages of finishing fulltime work is that we have the time to care for and repair these relationships.

Intimacy with people who belong to us is very good for our health and wellbeing – so much so that, if you are alone or have very few members in your family group, we recommend that you 'adopt' or create a family for yourself. You need one. Find people you are happy to be around and have special caring relationships with. Yes, all these people take time. And yes, some or all of them can be trying sometimes. But your life will be the richer and healthier for it.

Finding old friends and getting new ones

We all lose touch with people over the years. Once we leave school and start to go our separate ways it's hard to stay in contact with childhood friends, especially if your parents move from the original family home. This pattern gets repeated at later schools and colleges. Then, in our very busy middle life, our energy is consumed by work and raising families. Before we know it, we're getting invitations to twenty-five and fifty-year reunions!

> The internet is a great help in finding 'lost' friends. Googling a name is usually a great start.

There is a treasure in friendships that we developed early in life. Those people know different aspects of us. Now is a great time to find and rekindle friendships with some of the people you knew when you were younger – school friends, early work colleagues, people who shared the struggle when you were bringing up families, and so on.

The internet is a great help in finding 'lost' friends. Googling a name is usually a great start. Finding one usually leads to more. Email and Facebook allow us to keep in touch, and to gather up old groups easily.

The quality of your days can be affected by the kind of people you spend time with. Just because you may not intend to work fulltime any longer doesn't mean that you shouldn't continue to meet wonderful people and have great relationships with them. Being on good, friendly terms with everyone from your local barista to the parish priest, from your postie to your lawyer, is a great recipe for making each and every day a good one. You may already have great people in your life; or you may be starting from scratch in a new location – no matter what your circumstances, think about continuing to add new and mutually beneficial relationships to your life all the time. This is not manipulative – far from it, as the relationship will ideally be useful and worthwhile for everyone. Your level of connection with others is the third element, along with your health and your finances, in the critical trio that makes life good.

You will no doubt already have lots of contacts. As much as possible, try not to lose them. Email makes this easier than ever. But all the old media work too – so don't forget about appropriate cards or letters, as the occasion arises. And you could even have a go with some of the new ones – Twitter, Facebook, LinkedIn and other social media may open up new avenues and interest groups.

> One of the biggest mistakes people make when they leave fulltime work is to narrow their social group rather than broaden it.

Cast your net widely, and make friends and acquaintances wherever you go. Find individuals and groups who share your hobbies, or the new interests you are undertaking. One of the biggest mistakes people make when they leave fulltime work is to narrow their social group rather than broaden it. You should have more time now to experiment with joining everything from gyms and sports clubs to community groups and service organisations. You can always leave if it doesn't work out. The message here is to be expansive rather than exclusive

– it's really important not to make life prematurely narrow. Now you have the time to connect with others, and make your life richer and better.

Good places to start connecting include:

- **joining a club** – for example a book club, or a special interest group on LinkedIn
- **forming a group** around a special interest, eg, walking, investment, art
- **writing a blog** and attracting like-minded followers
- **doing a course** – for example, politics or French
- **volunteering** – for example, Meals on Wheels, Victim Support, hospice visiting, adult literacy
- **getting season tickets** to games, plays or opera

Clearly, if you still intend to work then your network of friends, acquaintances and contacts is very important to your success in finding appropriate work and getting good recommendations. But you also need a big network of people in your life just for quality and enjoyment of life. One of our most important recommendations is to simply be nice to people. Talk to them. Assume you will want to know, and be on friendly terms with everyone you meet – until they prove you wrong!

Making My Time Happen

'How we spend our days is, of course,
how we spend our lives.'

Annie Dillard

Making big decisions

It's one thing knowing what you want; it's another thing altogether to make the decisions to bring it about.

We all make decisions all day long – trivial ones about what to eat, what to wear, how to spend time. We may make bigger ones, too, at work – committing money and other resources to large projects and long-term programmes. However, we see many people who are 'stuck' when it comes to making changes – even changes that they say they really want – in their own lives.

Why is this? Perhaps it's because we are so overwhelmed with choice in our modern world – even choosing which pot of yoghurt to buy could take hours at the supermarket! When we have so much choice, it can feel like any choice is making a mistake, so we dither. Likewise with information. We are deluged with data on a daily basis about how to organise our money; what to do about our appearance, health and fitness; how we should be in order to be acceptable and successful . . . You could spend your whole life just trying to live up to the ideals of the Sunday supplements!

All of these choices take a lot of our energy. They can divert and distract us from making the choices that really matter:

- How do you want to live?
- Who do you want to become?
- What do you need to change in order to move towards having the ideal life?

It's important to get back into the habit of making decisions about stuff that matters (as opposed to which brand of coffee you drink, or which brand of trainers you wear). All significant change starts with a decision. State your problem or issue clearly – for example:

- 'I hate my job.'
- 'I want to live in the country.'
- 'I want to do something useful.'
- 'I don't like how we treat each other.'

Even impossible problems are solvable when we recognise that all we need to do is make a tough decision. For example, if you wish to start a business you may need to sell your home to raise the needed capital; self-employment requires that you give up your generous salary and perks; moving to live by the sea demands that you leave your present community and must build a new one.

Even impossible problems are solvable when we recognise that all we need to do is make a tough decision.

It's rare that you will get much positive change without being willing to give up something else in your life. Some of the 'losses' have big price tags – like security, predictability, approval or comfort. When you are facing a major transition toward the life you want, you may have to give up the security of fulltime paid employment; the predictability of how your time is organised, and how much income you will have. You may also face losing the approval of friends and family – and you may even have to work hard to win the approval of your nearest and dearest!

And it may be uncomfortable. It is one thing to fantasise about change; it's quite another to make the tough decisions required for change. When you have spent a great deal of life so far making your world secure, predictable and comfortable it can be very hard to make a decision that puts all that in jeopardy. Yes, you hope that the future life will be even better, but there are no guarantees. Many forces will conspire to get you to forget about it all – after all, it's 'just building castles in the air', isn't it? You will be accused of having a midlife crisis; there will be gentle suggestions that you'll soon get over it, and so on.

Don't resile from the tough decisions – your (ideal) life depends on it! Here are some strategies to help you make tough decisions:

- **Gather all the relevant facts.** Don't overdo this, though, as you can get stuck just amassing new data.
- **Consider the worst-case scenario.** What would you do? Have an 'out', or a Plan B, as that can give you some comfort.
- **Think about how wonderful things will be when it all works out.** It's important to be positive and optimistic – without being a total Pollyanna.
- **Consider the consequences of not doing anything.** Most people regret what they have not done rather than what they did.
- **Confront whatever is holding you back.** What is stopping you? What exactly are you afraid of? How realistic is your fear?
- **Listen to your heart as well as your head.** Your feelings, your gut, your intuition have a role here as well as your logical, rational head.

Then decide, and go forward. Whatever you do, don't stay stuck in indecision. You will waste your best time and the most valuable of your life's energies. It's crunch time!

> Whatever you do, don't stay stuck in indecision.

Later is now

One of the traps of being young, healthy and reasonably successful is that you are beguiled into thinking that you have all the time in the world to get to your ideal life. It ain't true. Life has a way of overtaking us: we get older; we acquire responsibilities; our health deserts us; significant people in our lives, like partners and children, get tired waiting for us to change; we may even give up on ourselves. If you keep putting off making the changes that would make you happier, you will at best get older; and at worst, you will lose all chance of getting what you want.

No matter what age or stage you are at now, it's important not to defer the big choices and decisions for too long. Options narrow; doors close.

> It's important not to defer the big choices and decisions for too long.

It's easy to defer life: you wait until you have finished your education (which can take a decade or more nowadays); wait until you have paid off your home; wait until you are established or have 'made it' in a career sense; wait until you have 'enough' money. It's not that these are not important milestones. The problem is that we get into the habit of continually putting off living the life we want. As the decades pass, there is some urgency about deciding that the time is right to have things more on your terms.

Be very wary of excuses that keep recurring. It's easy to be busy. It's easy to convince yourself that the time is not right. It's easy to believe that you don't have enough money. But you may be just inventing excuses to avoid the important stuff – like how you are going to spend the rest of your life.

Take responsibility. Do it now.

> Be very wary of excuses that keep recurring. It's easy to be busy. It's easy to convince yourself that the time is not right.

Changing habits
one at a time

It's not easy to become wealthy, healthy, and wise about your My Time all at once. Your mindset and motivation to achieve the life you want are very important, but it's what you do that matters. Behaviour is what counts. Behaviour change is often a challenge, and it's best to tackle it bit by bit.

You will have an idea by now of where you need to make changes – to your finances, your health, your work, your relationships. Rather than trying to get it all right at once, it may pay to identify habits and routines that you can change one at a time. As this can take a lot of effort on your part, choose carefully and get a new behaviour well established before you try to take on too many more changes.

Invest in new behaviours now for your My Time tomorrow. If you don't train, you get no gain. Don't wait until you finish fulltime work. Yes, you will have the freedom then, but will you have the physical vitality, mental resilience, and emotional health to live the life you want if you wait any longer? Yes, you have to invest your money, too; but it's even more important to make sure that you will be in great physical, mental and emotional condition to enjoy life after work.

Identify some of the 'old' habits that you need to discard or change – things like pouring a drink, opening the fridge, going shopping; or consuming trivial media out of boredom and discontent. These kinds of things don't take away the pain – they just disguise and dull it momentarily – and in fact they undermine our chances of ever having great My Time.

We have to work hard to find ways to replace these habitual default behaviours with new routines that will give us some better time right away, and give us the best chance of having decades of wonderful My Time. You probably know what you need to give priority to. Our interviewees noted that they made simple (if not easy to do!) changes such as:

- getting a dog (has to be walked)
- buying smaller plates (eating less)
- putting in a vege garden (eating better)
- joining LinkedIn (making connections)
- getting more sleep (managing energy).

Many also stepped up their focus on husbanding their finances – substituting mindless expenditure with mindful spending, and simplifying their lives in the process.

Think of all of these assets – your healthy body, vigorous mind and bright spirit, your energy for work, your enthusiasm for life and your financial wealth – as resources. Money alone won't give you the My Time you want; and it's not the only resource (or even the most important, perhaps) you have. All these resources must be cared for, nurtured and grown wherever possible if you are to get a long and satisfying My Time.

So keep reminding yourself why you want it. Take action in the areas where you can make change. Give yourself constant nudges in the right direction for the sake of your wellness and wealth. Find the habits you need to stop, start, change or maintain. Keep nudging in the direction of the My Time you want. Some things will get better immediately.

What can go wrong?

Our interviewees' experience is that change goes wrong at times. From their experience, we could pick out the following:

The unprepared.

They leap before they look. It's great that you are enthusiastic about getting the life you want; however, optimism isn't quite enough of a recipe for big change. Find out as much as you can about what you are leaping into. For example, don't move location on a whim, or go to a place that you have only been to in the high season. It's important to prepare the ground for change, and the many aspects of My Time need separate strategies – it's not a single thing. You need strategies for stimulation and challenge (which probably include work), for leisure, for relationships, for funding and for fitness.

> **Don't move location on a whim, or go to a place that you have only been to in the high season.**

The unaware.

They don't know themselves very well. You are seeking the ideal life-style for you, so it needs to fit around who you are. For example, if you have always enjoyed working in a big group with lots of activity and support, it's unlikely that you will enjoy being a self-employed consultant based at home.

The selfish.

They don't consider their partner's views. It's not that uncommon for people to approach major change without involving their spouse – like the chap who came home and announced that he had resigned his senior corporate job and that they were now the proud owners of a motel in Queenstown. It was the first she had heard of it, and she wasn't exactly pleased!

> It's not that uncommon for people to approach major change without involving their spouse.

The disconnected.

These people have had poor relationships. Having someone to love, and someone who loves you, seems to be essential for most people. Retirement often reveals the fracture lines in relationships that are covered over by the 'busy-ness' of fulltime work. Some couples have never adjusted to the 'empty nest', and the end of fulltime work forces them to confront it finally. This is not a great time of life to find out that your relationship is in tatters.

The closed down.

They are disconnected from their feelings. Most of what we read and hear about retirement is based on 'head' issues such as investment, living off capital, lifestyle communities and leisure activities. These are important, but they don't address the underlying fears and feelings about the change. Failure to examine, confront and address these feelings may mean that the change actually comes as a big shock. This can lead to feelings of alienation and depression, preventing you from enjoying your new life.

The ambivalent.

They don't know what they really want. It's hard to get what you want if you have no idea what it is. People who remain in denial about the end of their fulltime career often fail to spend enough time considering what they want for the rest of their lives. Others' timetables and wishes take over, and they can miss the opportunity to make sure they get at least some of what they want.

The runner.

They want to get away from something, rather than move towards something – pushed rather than pulled. Not everyone who retires liked their work, where they lived or their lifestyle. They may have been yearning to break the constraints of fulltime work for years. However, you still need a view of the future. You are unlikely to be satisfied staying in a vacuum for long. After a few weeks or months of leisure – and maybe a cruise or a world trip – you will still be in need of a new and satisfying existence.

The grass is greener.

They didn't appreciate what they had and are now leaving. It's human nature to take for granted what we have – whether it's the structures and routines around our work and our week; or the neighbourhood we live in, and the friends and amenities that go with it. These people are wired up to see mostly what is wrong – for example, Auckland traffic. We often forget what's readily available until we lose it – for example, the theatres, libraries, shows and good restaurants that we enjoyed in the city may be unavailable in the idyllic coastal settlement we're relocating to.

The isolated.

They have no network. Maybe this should be much higher on the list. It's very easy to take networks for granted when you still work full-time – you know lots of people by default. The more senior you are the more effortless it is. This all changes in an instant when you are no longer 'in power' or seen to be essential to others' career ambitions. This can mean that you are lonely, perhaps depressed, and even offended. More importantly, it can mean you lack the necessary networks to thrive in whatever it is you want to do next. You risk being lonely if you have not developed relationships outside work with family and friends.

> You risk being lonely if you have not developed relationships outside work with family and friends.

The misfit.

They moved location without thinking and testing first. Some people like kamikaze action – risking all on a big play. However, most major changes take a lot of detailed planning to get the basics right. For example, those contemplating a relocation need to spend time in their preferred destination, figuring out what life is like there all year round, making friends and getting involved with the local networks and community. Living fulltime somewhere is very different from visiting for a few weeks at peak season.

The exhausted.

They thought they'd be happy doing 'nothing', as they were overworked or burnt out. Almost no one enjoys doing nothing. This is especially true as more and more of us retire from fulltime work at a younger age and in better condition than the generations before us. Pretty much everybody needs something to do, someone to love and something to look forward to.

> Pretty much everybody needs something to do, someone to love and something to look forward to.

The naysayer.

They have a negative attitude – everything's a problem! Anyone can find problems if they are looking for them. There's plenty to complain about when change is afoot; and most of us dislike any change that is not of our choosing. However, it's important to have a good attitude – nothing marks us out as unappealing, yesterday people more than a critical, complaining, curmudgeonly style!

The unimaginative.

These people are closed-minded, and will only consider a narrow range of options. This can lead to prejudging and negativity about the form your life will take. This is a shame, given that we have more options now about how we live post retirement than any previous generation ever had.

The risk-averse.

One of the downsides of all of the negative talk about the perils of retirement is that some people feel very risk-averse. They are afraid they will not have enough, or that relocation or a change in lifestyle will be a disaster. No risk, no reward.

The rigid.

They are inflexible about what they will do and who they will associate with. It's tempting to start with a list of what you won't do and who you won't associate with. However, now is a great time for experimenting – and you might be pleasantly surprised.

The people pleaser.

This person is trying to please all of the people all the time – an impossible task. Even worse, their own needs are often overlooked or left until last. Now is the time to do what is right for you and meet your own needs. It's okay to please yourself!

Value your My Time

At this stage of life many people are very anxious about their resources – and they usually mean their money. Do they have enough? Will it last? What about inflation, etc? However, the resource you really need to budget is your time.

> The resource you really need to budget is your time.

You may have waited for decades – it may seem like all your life – to have some My Time. But if you're not careful, your time can evaporate or be siphoned off by others.

Fulltime work is a great excuse for saying 'no' to things you don't want to do, people you don't want to see, occasions you don't care to attend. Now, if you give up fulltime work, you may find yourself without excuses. Be prepared for this! Your partner may have plans for you that you want no part of. Your grown-up children may decide you are a handyperson or an unpaid babysitter. All kinds of people and groups and organisations may solicit your services. You might be delighted by this – and if so, go to it! However, if you suspect that you are about to be overwhelmed with invitations or requests that you don't want, be ready with your own plan for your My Time.

Try to learn how to say 'No'. If that's a problem for you, get ready with your excuses – organise some work, join something else quickly, or enrol in some study that you can claim hours of time for. The core message here is to make sure that your time goes where you wish. You have earned this. Think carefully about the routines you want, and your priorities. Make sure that your time to rest, read, exercise, reflect, play, work at your hobbies, etc, is all in the timetable before you let others steal your time. It's not just your hours they are taking – it's your dreams, and your My Time!

Quiz: Are you ready for My Time?

This may seem like a silly question: 'Am I ready?' you ask incredulously. 'I'm gasping!'

Our experience however is that though many people are highly motivated to stop whatever they are doing or change down a gear or two, there are many other things that need to be considered if you are to have good My Time. Any form of retirement, full or partial, means a considerable change. At the moment you may only be focused on what you wish to be rid of rather than what else you will need in your life. Take our quiz.

Are you ready for life after fulltime work?

1   Do you live a fairly well balanced life?

2   Do you have an annual health check?

3   Do you have close friends you feel you can rely on?

4   Do you have an active social life?

5　Do you do any voluntary or community work?

6　Do you have a spiritual dimension to your life?

7　Do you like learning new things, eg, languages, technology?

8　Are your hobbies and interests a large part of your life?

9　Have you got a 'bucket list' of things you want to do?

10　Do you use professional coaches, eg, life, financial?

11　Do you have a plan for life after work?

12　Do you know where you will live?

13　Do you and your partner have a shared dream about the future?

14　Do you and your partner talk about life after work?

15　Have you told your adult children about your plans?

16　Do you feel you have 'enough' funds to cease fulltime work?

17　Do you know yourself well enough to make good choices for you?

18　Do you think you have a good sense of the changes you can expect in the future?

19　Are you aware of the satisfactions you get from your work?

20　Do you have a plan for replacing work satisfactions if you give up working?

The more of these you can say yes to, the nearer you are to really enjoying My Time.

16–20 Just need a tune up. Congratulations! You are well on the way to having very fulfilling My Time.

11–15 Need a little work. You are steaming ahead. You sound as if you have many things in place to give you great quality of life. Select the areas you haven't addressed yet and work on getting even better My Time.

6–10 Unready for My Time. Still stuck? You seem to be immersed in your current role. However, if you have read this far you are obviously interested in how you can move to having more My Time. Pick out the areas that seem most important to you – for example, talking with your partner, or having a health check – and get started on getting a better life for you.

1–5 Urgent! You have us worried! We think you are probably drowning in your work and other responsibilities. We think you could pick one small change that you can make immediately to get you started on getting a scrap of My Time.

A final note

Martin Buber, a philosopher, wrote:

> Every person born in this world represents something new, something that never existed before, something original and unique and every man's foremost task is the actualization of his unique, unprecedented and never-recurring possibilities.

Get the My Time you want. Make it count. *Go make the rest of life the best of life.* And let us know how you get on.

www.mytime.co.nz
contact@my-time.co.nz